Patterns of Celebration

Patterns of Celebration

Layers of Meaning
in the Structure of the Eucharist

Paul Gibson

with songs by
The Common Cup Company

Anglican Book Centre
Toronto, Canada

1998
Anglican Book Centre
600 Jarvis Street
Toronto, Ontario
M4Y 2J6

Canadian Cataloguing in Publication Data

Gibson, Paul, 1932-
   Patterns of celebration: layers of meaning in the structure of the eucharist with songs by the Common Cup Company

ISBN 1-55126-190-1

1. Lord's Supper—Anglican Church of Canada. I. Title.

BX5149.C5G53 1997   264'.03036   C97-932507-2

CONTENTS

Foreword 7
    * *Draw the circle wide* 11

Gathering 13
    * *Come to the well* 25
    * *Wake! Wake from your sleep!* 27

Telling the Story 28
    * *Israel, wait for the morning* 39
    * *Mary laid her baby down* 40
    * *Cry Alleluia* 43

Prayers of the People 44
    * *Celtic prayer* 54
    * *So softly I'm fading* 56

The Table 57
    * *Invitation* 77
    * *Till you come* 79

Ungathering 80
    * *More than we can ask or imagine* 99
    * *A little child* 101

* Hymns

FOREWORD

The texts that follow are based on presentations on the liturgy that I prepared for the 1996 summer session of the Sorrento Centre on Shuswap Lake in British Columbia, where individuals and families are offered a range of educational and recreational opportunities. I was teamed during this week-long event with the Common Cup Company, a group of musicians who write, compose, perform, lead, and record songs on Christian life and insight.[1] Gordon Light, a member of the Common Cup Company, worked with me on my portion of the planning, and with other members of the group on their share of the common task.

Gordon and I began to work together on this project shortly after the fifth International Anglican Liturgical Consultation had met in Dublin. The Consultation and its findings were very much in my mind, particularly the emphasis it had placed on the *structure* of the eucharist and the basic division of that structure into five sections (gathering the community, telling and hearing the story, interceding, eating and drinking, and sending). In addition to the liturgical principles it reflects, this five-fold division was convenient because our program at Sorrento was divided into five major working sessions. We agreed to use the five elements of the eucharistic structure to try to help people understand the flow and pattern of the rite, and through that understanding to grasp its theological implications and move towards some vision of its meaning for parish, social, and personal life.

I find it hard to imagine a closer theological and liturgical "fit" than I experienced with the Common Cup Company. We began each session with song, moved into my presentation and a period

---

[1] The members of the Common Cup Company are Jim Uhrich, Ian Macdonald, Bob Wallace, and Gordon Light.

of small-group reflection, and then returned to a more extended, concluding period of song. Again and again the choice of songs and their themes indicated that the Common Cup Company had been moving on a track parallel to more formal and academic liturgical thought, especially as I have participated in it. But the major benefit for us all was that our combined approach enabled us to work at the issues in a truly *holistic* way (I use that overworked word to stand for the ability of the whole to accomplish more than the sum total of its parts in isolation), with alternation of right-brain and left-brain activity, of intuition and thought, poetry and prose—all bound together in the primordial, fundamental, pre-rational activity of song.

My texts were written for public presentation by *me*. I have tried to edit them for private reading by *others*. They were also intended to provide springboards and doorways for more informal reflection of which there is no written record. Some of the sideroads we pursued at Sorrento may consequently be missing in the material that follows. On the other hand, some new material has certainly been added, not least because two issues beg a more expanded treatment. The first is the question of who may receive communion, and especially the status of the unbaptized when they find themselves at a eucharistic celebration. The second is the role of irony in early Christian theology, and the possibility that our understanding of that irony may help us to get beyond some of the theological impasses that have plagued later Christians in general and Anglicans in particular.

I am indebted to an article by Gordon Lathrop, Schieren Professor of Liturgy at Lutheran Theological Seminary in Philadelphia, Pennsylvania, which has helped me to realize the symbolic, non-literal quality of early Christian references to sacrifice in relation to worship, and especially in regard to the eucharist, a quality that quite reverses the interpretation with which later generations burdened that notion, whether positively or negatively. My own reflection has led from Professor Lathrop's use of the category of *symbol* towards understanding a whole range of early Christian terminology as *ironic*, a theme that I have tried to develop later in these texts. In the meantime,

Professor Lathrop's thought has expanded along parallel lines.[2] I hope my dependence on him is clear in some of what follows, that his contributions to this line of inquiry are adequately acknowledged, and that nothing of mine with which he might disagree appears in any way to be attributed to him.

I have a sense that some of what follows might evoke a two-fold charge that I am reducing the gospel to mere humanism. If this happened, I would make a two-fold response. First, *No*, I stand too much in awe of the mystery of being, whether conceived in terms of theological symbol or human psychology or any other system of thought, to say, "This is *only* that," or "This may be *reduced* (explained, exhausted, gutted) to that." I reject a liberalism that is merely reductionist. I cannot tell what light the gospel diamond will refract for other pilgrims in another day, nor can I deny the vision that such light may illumine for them, simply because it is not identical to mine. There can be no final reduction of the gospel to one system of interpretation, however authoritative. The shadow side of General Councils is that they are called to deal with current emergencies, but they then make decisions that are binding forever. The gospel speaks to each context, and we must struggle to hear it in and for our own context.

But *Yes*, I am proclaiming the gospel as humanism—*divine* humanism. For me, the essence of the prophetic and evangelical message is that *God is for humanity*, for human freedom and fulfillment—a staggering reversal of the familiar religious assumption that humanity exists for God. In fact, the gospel goes further and suggests that whatever we mean by *God* is known in and through the limitations and ambiguities of human life, especially as it is experienced at the levels of insecurity and alienation among the "least" of humanity.[3] The life, person, teaching, program, and disastrous but ultimately effective career of Jesus of Nazareth models (reveals) this.

---

[2] See his important *Holy Things: A Liturgical Theology*, Augsburg Fortress, Minneapolis, 1993.

[3] Matthew 25.40

I have asked the publishers to print the notes to this book on the pages to which they refer. In my opinion and experience, *endnotes* are not intended for reading: they "cover" the author and publisher against charges of plagiarism or piracy. *Footnotes*, on the other hand, extend the conversation sideways into directions that might confuse the main central thread of the discussion but that may interest and engage some readers. They also suggest opportunities for further reading. They are an auxiliary part of the work.

My thanks to Barbara Liotscos, who read these texts more than once and suggested many helpful improvements in both presentation and content.

My thanks to Minka Sprague, who advised me on a point of biblical exegesis.

My thanks again to the members of the Common Cup Company with whom I worked at Sorrento: Ian Macdonald, Bob Wallace, Gordon Light, and (for this occasion) Martha Graham, and to the wonderful people who turned up each day to listen, to engage in shared reflection, and to sing. Discourse floats on the river of attention.

Draw the circle wide

Keyboard intro.

(wide.) Draw the cir - cle wide. Draw it wid - er

still. Let this be our song, no one stands a -

lone, stand-ing side by side, draw the cir - cle

Fine

wide.
1 God the still - point of the cir - cle,
2 Let our hearts touch far hor - i - zons,
3 Let the dreams we dream be larg - er

'round whom all cre - a - tion turns; noth-ing lost, but
so en - com-pass great and small; let our lov - ing
than we've ev - er dreamed be - fore; let the dream of

D.C. al Fine

held for - ev - er, in God's gra - cious arms.
know no bor - ders, faith - ful to God's call.
Christ be in us, o - pen ev - ery door.

Text and music: Gordon Light. © *The Common Cup Company.*

GATHERING

*S*everal years ago my wife and I spent part of our vacation in a small village in southern France where an eastern rite Catholic community had taken over a medieval abbey. Early each morning I went down to the abbey church and joined the community there in a form of morning prayer that was built mostly around the great doxological hymns that conclude the psalter. On the one Sunday that we were in the village, we went to the eucharistic liturgy, arriving a few minutes early to get our bearings.

The church appeared to be in great confusion. The choir was singing the end of morning prayer. The priest and deacon were still preparing the bread and wine for the procession in which the gifts would later be carried to the altar. Servers were moving through the congregation with trays on which they were collecting written intercessions. The very devout were moving from icon to icon, saying prayers and lighting candles. And then I was conscious of the deacon taking his place between the altar and the people, and the priest standing at the holy table. Everyone seemed to have moved to the place where they ought to be. There was a hush like the corporate intake of a breath, a moment of brief but powerful silence. Almost in an undertone, the deacon invited the priest to give the blessing, and in a loud voice the priest intoned, *"Béni soit le royaume du Père, et du fils, et du Saint Esprit, maintenant, et toujours, et dans les siècles des siècles"* (Blessed be the kingdom of the Father, and of the Son, and of the Holy Spirit, now, and forever, and to the ages of ages). The people responded with a polyphonic, "Amen," and like a great ship leaving harbour and gathering speed in the tidal current, the liturgy moved into the weekly voyage of praise, supplication, and thanksgiving, the rhythmic act of worship (honour) that the people of God bring to the source and centre of their being.

BEGINNING WITH BLESSING

We are used to a liturgy *ending* with a blessing; in fact, we expect it and are surprised when it doesn't happen. We are less used to a liturgy *beginning* with a blessing. I think this is because we have a real but limited view of blessing. We think of a blessing as a gift, something given us to take away. We think of a blessing as a gesture that enhances the person or object over which it is invoked, that somehow adds holiness to that which was not so holy before. The eastern mind is closer to the Jewish roots of blessing. In Jewish theology it is not people and things that are blessed but God. People bless God for the gifts of life, the day, food, anniversaries; and it is in the act of blessing that these things that come decked in holiness from the Creator's hand are released for our use.[4] The Byzantine liturgy *begins* with a blessing of the reign of God, and so the worshippers who are already inheritors of God's realm are released to find their places once again in the kingdom as it is made present in symbol.

LAWS OF LITURGICAL CHANGE

One of the great liturgical scholars of the early part of this century was a man named Anton Baumstark, who is remembered now chiefly for his book, *Comparative Liturgy*. Baumstark's study suggests that there are number of principles or laws that govern the development and revision of liturgy, and that it is important to know what they are if your engagement with liturgy is to be more than mindless tinkering. One principle is that *liturgies tend to move from simplicity to complexity*.[5] From one point of view, this

---

[4] See Lawrence Hoffman, "Blessings and Their Translation in Current Jewish Liturgies," *Worship*, March 1986, vol. 60, no. 2, pp. 134–161.

[5] "If we now pass to the examination of the liturgical texts themselves we find that here, too, development proceeds from simplicity and brevity towards ever greater richness and ploxity." A. Baumstark, *Comparative Liturgy*, Eng. tr. ed. F.L. Cross, A.R. Mowbray and Co. Ltd., London, 1958, p. 20.

means that liturgies become richer and more varied. From another point of view, however, it means that they are inclined (like my basement) to attract clutter. People are constantly inventing new practices that they believe will make their worship more pastorally sensitive, more open to certain types of piety, deeper, broader, whatever. And so they add a new element to the fabric of their existing worship—a "children's chat," a welcome, a theme statement, a procession, an extra hymn—and the liturgy gradually becomes more and more complicated.

Another of Baumstark's principles is that reform eventually happens and it involves trimming, but *the older rather than the newer material tends to be pruned.*[6] If you really have to make a place in the program for a children's pageant, you might decide to skip the reading from the Old Testament, in spite of the fact that reading from the Jewish scriptures was standard practice throughout the church for about the first six centuries, and that it protects Christians from losing sight of the gospel's deep roots in the salvation history of the common tradition. I was once told about a priest who sometimes recognized that he had preached too long. In order to end the service on something like the intended schedule he would prepare the bread and wine and then tell the congregation, "We will use only the essential words today," skipping all of the eucharistic prayer except the description of the last supper. He didn't realize that the thanksgiving element in the prayer is more than probably older than the use of the words attributed to Jesus, and that one ancient Christian tradition seems to have had the prayer but not the description of what Jesus did at the last supper.

---

[6] Baumstark, op. cit., p. 23f, "In general, because the primitive elements are not immediately replaced by completely new ones, the newcomers at first take their place alongside the others. Before long they assume a more vigorous and resistant character, and when the tendency to abbreviation makes itself felt it is the more primitive elements which are the first to be affected: these disappear or leave only a few traces."

PURPOSE OF A LITURGICAL ACTION

It is not my purpose to argue that in a time of reform we should always retain the old and abandon the new. That would be mere archaeologism, which is a liturgical vice. I do, however, suggest that it is worth asking which parts of a liturgy are older and what those who originally shaped and adopted them were trying to do with them. It is worth asking whether our innovations are consistent with that earlier design. And if we decide that our latest insight is far better than the earlier model, we should decide in its favour intentionally and with an informed mind, and not simply on the basis of whim. The older tradition may at least help us understand what a section or gesture of the liturgy was for, and that will help us decide if it is a good thing to do and how we can do it most effectively ourselves.

A few years ago I participated in a meeting of native and non-native church leaders who had been asked to discuss inculturation and develop a statement. (By inculturation, I mean the growth of a liturgical form from within a culture, as distinct from its imposition from outside.) In a conversation over lunch with a First Nations priest, I suggested that a major purpose of the first part of the eucharist was to shape the community and bring it together. I said to him that in my culture we have tended to model our gathering rite on a public meeting: the president calls the meeting to order, and the participants, who have been engaged in their own thoughts and perhaps even in conversations among one another, give their attention. "How do *you* form a gathering of people into a community?" I asked. He said, "We make a circle." And then he added, "And it is very hard to do that in the long narrow buildings you have given us."

I hope that if the priest with whom I had that lunchtime conversation ever works on a liturgy from within his own culture he will not start by translating either the opening section of the Prayer Book eucharist or the Gathering Rite in the *Book of Alternative Services* (together with their respective rubrics) into Cree. I hope he will start by asking, "What is our opening rite *for?*" If he looks at ancient rites, I hope he will ask, "What were these people trying to do?" and "Can we do something similar in our own way?"

THE DEVELOPMENT OF GATHERING RITES

The oldest evidence suggests that people took their gathering for granted. Justin Martyr, who provides the earliest detailed description we have of a full Sunday service, says only, "On the day which is called the day of the sun there is an assembly of all who live in the towns or in the country; and the memoirs of the Apostles or the writings of the prophets are read, as long as time permits."[7] Actually, there is a point well into the Byzantine liturgy when the priest leaves the sanctuary by a side door and carries the gospel book in procession to the main door of the sanctuary. (Byzantine churches have a screen with three doors, which separates the sanctuary from the nave.) "Wisdom!" cries the priest. "Let us stand!" Hymns are sung, and then the epistle and gospel are read. Some scholars think that this carrying of the book into the assembly is the original beginning of the rite, the original focal gesture that brought the community together.

Dom Gregory Dix, in his imaginative reconstruction of an early liturgy, pictures a congregation of early Christians gathering in the drawing room of a wealthy member of their community during the early dawn of a Sunday morning. A deacon scrutinizes them at the door, not least because their assembly is illegal and they will do well to avoid the presence of informers. The bishop, an elderly gentleman in middle-class clothes, sits in an armchair at the end of the room. The community's committee—the presbyters—sit in a semi-circle on either side. "The eucharist is

---

[7] Henry Bettenson, *Documents of the Christian Church*, Oxford University Press, New York, 1947, p. 94.
[8] G. Dix, *The Shape of the Liturgy*, Dacre Press, Adam and Charles Black, London, 1945, p. 142.

about to begin. The bishop stands and greets the church. At once there is silence and order, and the church replies."[8] As late as the time of Augustine (fifth century), the liturgy began with a greeting and the reading of the lections.[9]

Clearly Christians did not remain satisfied with the original simplicity of the opening of their services. In the Byzantine East, litanies, prayers, and anthems were added, reducing the original entrance (as I have described) to a peculiar walk out of one door in the screen (called the *iconostasis*), across the front of the church, and into another door. In the West, the hymn *Gloria in Excelsis* was added, as well as the chant *Kyrie eleison, Christe eleison* (which may or may not have been the responses to the suffrages of a now-vanished litany), a formal prayer that varied from celebration to celebration, a variable entrance chant that was usually based on a psalm, and eventually prayers of the ministers at the foot of the altar, which included a recitation of Psalm 43 and forms of general confession. Josef Jungmann, the great student of the traditional Roman rite, readily admits that, "the thing that strikes us about the whole ceremonial, from the prayers at the foot of the altar to the collect, is its lack of coherence; we do not get the impression of something unified."[10]

It is not surprising that the opening section of the eucharist as designed by Cranmer in 1552 (the form that became more or less definitive for most subsequent Anglican prayer books) was no less confusing than the raw materials he had to work with. He transferred the Lord's Prayer and the Collect for Purity from the table of prayers recited by English priests while vesting to the opening point of the liturgy. He moved the *Gloria in Excelsis* to the end of the rite, thus depriving the opening section of a strong

---

[9]   J. Jungmann cites *De civ. Dei*, 22, 8, where Augustine describes an Easter day when a sick man was cured just before the eucharist began. Augustine was in the sacristy when the information was brought to him. When the excitement in the church finally became subdued, the bishop greeted the people and the reading of the scriptures followed immediately. C.f. Jungman, *The Mass of the Roman Rite*, vol. 1, Benziger Brothers, New York, 1951, p. 262.

[10]   Ibid., p. 266.

and unifying hymn of praise. He retained the *Kyrie* chant but, in the spirit of the didactic pedagogy of sixteenth-century humanism, he intercalated it with the ten commandments. Following the late medieval trend towards the multiplication of details, he abandoned the earlier practice of a single opening prayer and added a second collect for the king. In many ways he fell into the trap of Baumstark's second law: he knew a reform was needed, but he rearranged and attempted to rationalize the newer pattern of clutter rather than return to the original model of simplicity. And, most significantly, he retained and strengthened in the opening rite a late medieval emphasis on inner and personal preparation of the individual, where earlier patterns had emphasized the beginning of the eucharist as the coming together of a community.

REFORM OF GATHERING RITES

The reform of liturgical texts in the twentieth century has moved towards some recovery of both the original simplicity and the original function of the opening rite. The opening section of the eucharist in the *Book of Alternative Services* is clearly labelled, "The Gathering of the Community." It was intended by the Doctrine and Worship Committee that prepared it to be composed ordinarily of three elements: a greeting, a hymn of praise, and a focusing prayer.[11] The *Gloria, Kyrie eleison*, and *Trisagion* were provided as alternative and traditional acts of praise, but a rubric makes it quite clear that another canticle or hymn may be used. The act of praise is itself optional (although it is obviously encouraged), and the gathering rite may consist of the greeting, an invitation to pray, a few moments of common silence, and the prayer of the day.

---

[11] The Collect for Purity, representing later medieval preoccupation with personal and inner piety, was reinserted into this scheme by an act of the House of Bishops. The Committee had retained it as a psalm prayer for Psalm 51.

Once there are options in the way the gathering rite may be done, we are left with the question, "How should *we* do it?" And questions that ask "How?" imply questions that ask "What are we trying to achieve?" The way in which we gather is filled with questions, and they are theological questions whose answers may define our understanding and interpretation of all else that happens. If the gathering is essentially a conspicuous and flamboyant procession of choir and clergy, we may be defining the liturgy as a sanctuary event at which the people are primarily spectators. If it is dominated by announcements of a domestic nature, we may be defining the liturgy as the property of an in-group where strangers are welcome officially but not really. (I used to belong to a congregation where anyone who wished could go to the pulpit during the gathering rite and make an announcement: this once took 25 minutes.) If, as in one congregation where I occasionally worship, the most conspicuous element in the gathering rite is the dismissal of the children to their Sunday School, we may be making a profound statement about the equality of the members of the baptized community.[12]

A THEOLOGY OF GATHERING

What are we trying to do in the gathering rite? I have already intimated that we are calling a community into conscious, active identity. Let me amplify that proposal.

The gathering rite calls together an assembly of the baptized. It is, in fact, a bridge between the end of the baptism liturgy and the beginning of the eucharistic liturgy. There is (to paraphrase the letter to the Ephesians) not only one Lord and one faith but

---

[12] The first item in the Principles and Recommendations of the Fifth International Anglican Liturgical Consultation (Dublin, 1995) reads, "In the celebration of the eucharist, all the baptized are called to participate in the great sign of our common identity as the people of God, the body of Christ, and the community of the Holy Spirit. No baptized person should be excluded from participating in the eucharistic assembly on such grounds as age, race gender, economic circumstance or mental capacity."

also *one* baptism, one single sea of water through which we all have passed. There is, theologically, no such thing as *my* baptism or *your* baptism; there is the baptism of the people of God. Although I am a distinct human being, I do not have a private humanity; I am a human being because I share in the humanity of all people. Just so, I am a Christian because I share in the baptism of all Christians. The community is constituted by that crisis event (as humanity is constituted in the crisis event of being born), with its images of death, life, drowning, rescue, healing, and cleansing. Every eucharist begins where baptism left off—we arrive as if soaking wet—and some of our modern rites are open to expressing this. The baptism liturgy in the *Book of Alternative Services* ends with the congregational greeting of the newly-baptized: "We receive you into the household of God. Confess the faith of Christ crucified, proclaim his resurrection, and share with us in his eternal priesthood." The eucharist always begins at this point, the calling of the household of God into its shared activity in the eternal priesthood of the Lord, and the rite should make this clear.

THE GATHERED CHURCH AS EVENT

The gathering rite assembles the Christian community as an *event* that is the icon of God's reign, God's kingdom. This relationship between the Christian community and the reign or kingdom of God is very important. It is also very tricky, not because it is difficult but because its misunderstanding and consequent misuse may lead the church into deformities of message and practice.

There are two points we must grasp. First, it is important to recognize that God's reign or kingdom is experienced in events and relationships and not as a commodity or *thing* that may be possessed or owned. In the teaching of Jesus, the kingdom of God has an elusive quality. God's kingdom belongs to the poor[13]

---

[13] Luke 6.20

and to children and to those who are like them,[14] but it is not easily entered by the rich.[15] God's reign is not open to ordinary methods of observation.[16] Jesus' teaching about the kingdom is mostly in terms of what it is *like* rather than what it *is*—it is like a mustard seed, or yeast in a batch of dough, or treasure hidden in a field, or a great banquet. It is certainly not like the Roman Empire. It is already *among* Jesus' hearers, not over them.[17] It is important for us to distinguish between events in which the kingdom of God may be apprehended and any suggestion that the kingdom of God may be described as a *thing* that can be held or measured or even (God forbid!) controlled.

Second, when we talk about the church as witness or sign of God's kingdom, we must be doubly careful not to suggest that the church as organization or institution or corporate entity in some way *is* the kingdom. When the church identifies itself with God's kingdom, so as to suggest that it *is* the kingdom as an object or *thing*, it is in danger of the corporate equivalent of ego-inflation—self-assurance becoming arrogance becoming insensitivity becoming power and control. The kingdom of God cannot be owned like property. On the contrary, we can only participate in events that open us to its possibility, at that moment and in the rest of our lives. Our acts of worship are such events. Indeed, the church is best understood not as a static entity or *thing* at all, but as a continuous event—a string (or chain or cord) of events—witnessing to the reign of God and opening us to its possibility. The gathering rite should articulate this.

If the reign of God is our true home, then the gathering of the community should suggest the experience of "coming home." We do not *go* to church; we *come home* to church. We belong here, because the truth and beauty we meet here are the proper environment of the rest of our lives.

---

[14] Luke 18.16
[15] Mark 10.23–25
[16] Luke 17.20
[17] Luke 17.21

PRACTICAL CONSIDERATIONS

How we gather will vary from congregation to congregation, from occasion to occasion. But it should never be taken for granted. Although its basic structure may, as the *Book of Alternative Services* suggests, consist of a greeting, an act of praise, and a prayer, other elements may be added so long as they are adopted and fashioned with care and with an eye on the integrity of the action.

For instance, there is no need for the presider to say, "Good morning," before greeting the people with the grace of our Lord Jesus Christ, because the words, "The grace of our Lord Jesus Christ, the love of God, and the fellowship of the Holy Spirit be with you all," are a formal and biblical way of saying, "Hello." On the other hand, a more informal welcome may be woven into basic announcements after the opening greeting—and basic announcements may be needed.

An opening hymn, before anything else happens, may be necessary for tradition's sake, but the traditional procession should not be taken for granted, and the use of an opening hymn as the act of praise after the greeting should be considered.

Sometimes a statement of the principal concern of the day may be helpful (the *Book of Alternative Services* provides for this in the marriage eucharist, for instance). But there is no room in the opening rite for gimmicks. The tendency of the opening and closing sections of the liturgy to attract clutter should never be forgotten. Every addition should be examined for its effectiveness in bringing the community and its purpose into focus.

The flavour of the gathering rite may change from time to time—seasonally, and in terms of the situation of the people involved. For instance, the shadow side of praise is lament, and there are times to stress the lament dimension of that tension—seasons like Lent, and occasions like funerals, and times of parting and sadness. (The *Book of Alternative Services* provides a penitential order for use in Lent, and other appropriate occasions, at which the ten commandments and other suitable selections of scripture may be read.) But the most developed lament psalms (like 22) tend to conclude with a hymn of praise and hope, and the hope that is the vocation of the assembly should not be forgotten.

All of this requires sensitivity to the people involved, to the occasion, to the readings and prayers that will follow. The gathering rite is not just a way of getting started; it is a statement of the theology of all that follows.

FOR DISCUSSION

Members of your family, who have been separated for a long time, are coming for Christmas. How could you arrange Christmas dinner so that they really feel they are not just visitors but have, in a real sense, come home?

Come to the well

Come to the well, come to the wa-ters, come to the ri-ver ris-ing deep with-in your soul; come to the source of the life that God of-fers, come, fill your cup from the cool of the well. To st. 1–3 A well.

1–3 Em   4 G   *End*

1 place to share your sor-rows, a place to sing your song. A well of tears to wash your wounds, a place you can be - long;

2 place of hard en - count-er, trace the pat-terns of your days, a well of cleans-ing laugh-ter to take sin's weight a - way.

3 place of trans-for - ma - tion, weak-ness turns to strength, a well of hope to heal the hurt all through the jour-ney's length;

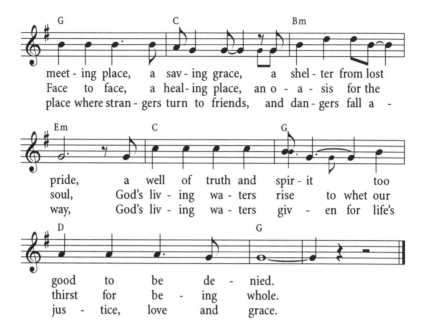

meet - ing place,   a   sav - ing   grace,   a   shel - ter from lost
Face   to   face,   a   heal - ing   place,   an o - a - sis   for the
place where stran - gers turn to   friends,   and dan - gers fall a -

pride,   a   well   of   truth and   spir - it   too
soul,   God's liv - ing   wa - ters   rise   to whet our
way,   God's liv - ing   wa - ters   giv - en for life's

good   to   be   de - nied.
thirst   for   be - ing   whole.
jus - tice,   love   and   grace.

Text: Ian Macdonald and Gordon Light.
Music: Gordon Light.

Text and music © The Common Cup Company.

Wake! Wake from your sleep!

Refrain

Wake! Wake from your sleep! Rise up from the dead!

Rise from the wa-ters deep! Christ in your heart and head!

1 His peace fill your heart;
2 His Spir-it fill your days;

his life for your own. His light shine
love's fire, ho-ly wind. His cross to

To refrain

in the dark and bring you safe-ly home.
mark your way, and lead to jour-ney's end.

Refrain may be sung as a round or canon after verse 2,
repeating measures 9 and 10 until all finish.

Text and music: Gordon Light. © *The Common Cup Company.*

TELLING THE STORY

PERSONALITY TYPE AND WORSHIP

*I*n recent years many people have found increased understanding of their own personalities and those of others through a device known as the Myers-Briggs Type Indicator. A profile of personality may be determined through an easy and non-threatening questionnaire that, when properly scored, locates an individual within the pattern of functions discerned by the philosopher-psychologist Carl Gustav Jung. This pattern contributes to the shape and dynamic of each personality.

Jung suggested that each of us prefers to respond to our various experiences of the world around us by

1   accepting what we experience (perceiving), or controlling and regulating it (judging),

2   using that inner experience first for ourselves and our own inner life (introversion), or impressing it on the world around us (extraversion),

3   broadening that experience through the activity of the mind (thinking), or through the response of the emotions (feeling), and

4   expanding our awareness through activity of the senses (sensing), or through an inner process of understanding (intuiting).

Each of us does all of these things, but we prefer to work in and through some of them rather than others. None of these ways of expressing our personalities is better or worse than the others, although sometimes a culture values one or other of them more than its counterpart. To some extent they are part of the package that we are born with, and to some extent they were acquired in the process of living.[18]

I have a strong feeling that not enough work has been done on the relationship of styles of worship and types of personality. If we find a style of worship with which we are comfortable, we tend to regard it as normative and wonder why some people seem to be critical of it. If we find a style of worship with which we are uncomfortable, we tend to avoid it. And if we are, like me, "judging" and "thinking" people, people who want to control and process the information that stimulates them by thinking about it, then we may try to find ways to explain to others why that form of worship is satisfactory or unsatisfactory, no matter how unconvincing our argument may be to them. Deep down, "introverted" and "intuitive" people are probably not going to be happy if you tell them they have to dance in church, and "extroverted" and "feeling" people are not going to enjoy an atmosphere in which they are required to analyze and discuss deep thoughts.

I hope that some painstaking research will be done in this field, for I suspect there are people with profound spiritual resources and deep spiritual needs who seldom if ever go to church, because they have not found a church where their personality type is addressed and expanded and where they are given opportunity for it to become the means of their growth. At the same time, I suspect there are churches that offer their regular members only a partial challenge, because they cater to their expressed needs alone, without sufficient reference to the wider human picture and the possibility of growth through attention to less-preferred styles of functioning.

To some extent Christians have farmed out their ministry to different personality types on a denominational basis. Anglicans have, perhaps, catered to introverts, Pentecostals to extroverts

---

[18]   There is a wealth of literature on this subject. I found the introductory material in Bruce Duncan's *Pray Your Way* (Darton, Longman and Todd, London, 1993) particularly helpful.

(to oversimplify grossly). And within our Anglican denomination we have, to some extent, catered to different personality types at different times of day. The quiet Prayer Book service at 8:00 in the morning may appeal to people with a strong intuitive orientation, providing an environment in which private reflection has free rein. A suburban "family eucharist" at 10:00 may give vent to feelings, expressed in exuberant hymns and in a sympathetic response to children interacting among themselves and with their families. Monastic communities address quite specifically the personality types attracted to their lifestyle. Their worship is often austere, filled with intuition-fertile silences. It frequently attracts outsiders of similar type who would never themselves join the religious life formally, but who are nevertheless part of its larger orbit. Thomas More, Chancellor of England under Henry VIII and a renowned "family man," is said to have bought his house in Chelsea because there was a Carthusian abbey nearby and he wanted to attend its liturgy regularly.

I hope that the future of any research that is undertaken into the relationship of personality types and styles of worship results in the consideration of two principles. First, *every liturgy should address in some way or another the rich spectrum of the personality types that make up the human race.* As Jesus said, in God's house are many rooms. Everyone who attends a liturgy, unless it has been designed for a very particular and specifically-defined community of people, should know that their form of expression is valued and that there is a place for them. I do not mean that we should have two minutes of intuitive worship and five minutes of extroverted worship, and so on. That would be silly. I mean that we should review our worship regularly and ask if it addresses the range of styles of human involvement.

My second principle is this: *no one should be coerced into forms of behaviour that are in conflict with their personality, or should feel disvalued, whether by criticism or by pity, because they are unable to worship against the grain of their personality type.* The worshipping assembly is an event where difference is to be esteemed, not discounted; it is a place for respect, not for domination. This is one of the basic meanings of the washing of feet at the last supper.

READING THE BIBLE IN LITURGY

Some "church growth" experts have counselled conventional churches to abandon their liturgical traditions and offer worship that is described as "people centred" in a much more immediately accessible form than traditional liturgies can offer.[19] One leader in this field has recommended the abandonment of traditional schemes for public reading of the Bible (lectionaries) in favour of shorter portions of scripture, which are likely to carry a more immediate impact and provide a platform for energetic preaching.

Perhaps the problem is not so much with a lectionary as a systematic scheme for public reading of the Bible but with the style of reading itself. Too often the Bible is read in church as though it were an exercise intended by and for intuitive, thinking personalities. Sometimes the style of reading is so reflective, so internal to the reader, that I wonder (as preacher) if the congregation will have heard (*really* heard) the text on which I am about to comment. If I read it again, will the reader be insulted? If I don't, will the people know what I am talking about?

The liturgy of the word provides an opportunity for readers to function as extraverts, even if that is not their preferred orientation, and for listeners to be encouraged to give free rein to their sensing function, even if that is not the way they normally operate. Can we see and hear the writers and speakers? Can we smell the crowds and the flowers of the fields, feel the radiant heat of Moses' burning bush, taste the tears of sorrow and joy of the exiles returning from Babylon? Not every liturgy must be an occasion of exhausting verisimilitude, but our senses should be

---

[19] This is scarcely a new technique: it was used by Bernard of Clairvaux, Francis of Assisi, Ignatius Loyola, and John Wesley, to name but a few representatives of various mission and evangelistic movements.

addressed by the vividness of the story.

STORY AS A BUILDING-BLOCK OF RELIGION

The key word here is *story*. Story is one of the basic building-blocks of religion. The *telling of the story* of a people, of creation, of the land, is performed not merely for educational or didactic purposes but as a ritual act, comparable to procession or sacrifice. Mircea Eliade points out that creation stories are told not just to inform the hearers of their origins but to bring them back to the primal beginning so that they may be created anew.[20] This is particularly the case when creation stories are told as part of a new year observance, as a ritual act that enables the people to start afresh, to be reborn. Eliade also documents the use of creation stories in healing rituals. The creation story of a people is recited over a sick person so that he can go back to the beginning and start over again, hopefully without the disease.[21] This primitive custom passed into Christianity. Chaucer, for instance, says of the friar in his *Canterbury Tales*, "Gracious was his *In principio*." The friar, a disreputable cleric who preyed on vulnerable women, apparently went about reciting the prologue to John's gospel for alms or whatever else he could get.

SALVATION IS THE BIBLE'S STORY

Christianity, and the Judaism which is its root, are above all a religion of *story*. Unlike the earlier religions, however, their primary story is not creation but salvation. The God of the Bible first of all heals and saves and, in doing so, creates a *people* through whom the world will be healed and saved.

---

[20] Mircea Eliade, *The Sacred and the Profane*, Harcourt, Brace and Company, Inc., 1959, p. 105.
[21] Ibid., pp. 80–85.

The *natural* creation stories of the Bible have a secularizing dimension: in a world in which the natural order was regarded as enchanted and the sun, moon, and stars were regarded as forces in control of human fate, the first creation story in Genesis tells its hearers that nature is not magical because all these things were made by God and have their functional place in the divine scheme. There is no need to be afraid of them because God has declared them good. Even Psalm 148, one of the most nature-oriented psalms of all, concludes with the words, "He has raised up strength for his people and praise for all his loyal servants, the children of Israel, a people who are near him." This raising up of the people is God's essential agenda.

The story of the Bible really begins with Genesis 12 and the call of Abraham to leave his country and people and go to a new land where God will make of him a great nation, "in whom all the families of the earth shall be blessed." This basic story is defined still further in Exodus 12 and its announcement, "This month shall mark for you the beginning of months." The importance of the telling of the story is defined in Exodus 12 and 13: "And when your children ask you, 'What do you mean by this observance?' you shall say, 'It is the passover sacrifice to the Lord, for he passed over the houses of the Israelites in Egypt, when he struck down the Egyptians .... You shall tell your child on that day, 'It is because of what the Lord did for me when I came out of Egypt.'"

This centrality of the story of salvation reaches its apex in the harvest festival rite of Deuteronomy 26 where the worshipper is told to bring some of the first fruit of the ground in a basket and take it to the worship place and declare to the priest, "A wandering Aramaean was my ancestor; he went down into Egypt and lived there as an alien .... When the Egyptians treated us harshly and afflicted us, by imposing hard labour on us, we cried to the Lord, the God of our ancestors; the Lord heard our voice and .... brought us out of Egypt with a mighty hand and an outstretched arm ... and brought us into this place." Telling the story and offering the first fruit combine to be an act of worship.

There is but one story in the Bible, the story of salvation and deliverance, sometimes seen through its shadow side of judgement and correction, but repeated often and in various forms. It appears not only in the story of the Exodus but also in the account of Israel's exile and return. The salvation story is amplified by the reflection of the prophets, not least in the dreams of a new and universal Exodus by the author of the middle section of the book we call *Isaiah*. Even Job is a story of personal salvation from a mixture of religious obsession and moral self-satisfaction.

The resurrection stories of the New Testament are also stories of deliverance, affirming not only that death has not driven Jesus into the past, but also celebrating the resurrection of his followers as the communal embodiment (incarnation) of his ministry. The seeds of this vision of resurrection were already present in the story of the salvation of the Hebrews from slavery in Egypt, enabling Paul in the language of Exodus to celebrate Christ as, "our Passover, [who] is sacrificed for us." This interpenetration of the old and new may go some distance towards explaining the curious line in Hippolytus's eucharistic prayer (the oldest complete eucharistic text available to us):

> When he was betrayed to voluntary suffering that he might destroy death, and break the bonds of the devil, and tread down hell, and shine upon the righteous, and fix a term, *and manifest the resurrection*, he took bread.[22]

It is for Hippolytus as though the resurrection had already existed, like a Platonic ideal or an eternal reality, and the self-giving of Jesus had revealed it with ultimate clarity. There is one story, and this is its heart.

It is interesting that both Jewish and Christian liturgical traditions have given primacy of place to the more narrative forms of their literary tradition. It is the *Torah*, the five scrolls that contain the stories of the call and redemption of the people,

---

[22] Geoffrey J. Cuming, *Hippolytus: A Text for Students*, Grove Books, Bramcote, Nottingham, 1976, p. 10f (italics mine).

which is housed in the ark and is given particular reverence when it is read in synagogue. And it is the gospel, the four books that contain the stories of the remaking of humanity in Christ, which is carried in procession and enthroned in the arms of an assistant while the lector chants it before a standing congregation. I have been present when the gospel book was carried through the congregation after the reading for worshippers to reach out and touch as it passed (a custom also observed with the *Torah* scroll in some synagogues). Both traditions assign a more subsidiary, explicatory role to the less narrative literature, whether the prophets and the writings among Jews, or the epistles among Christians. Of course, we now know that if earlier Christians cherished the notion that the gospel stories were somehow closer to Jesus and less filtered by theological speculation, they were quite wrong. The gospels are not the oldest portion of the Christian literary heritage, nor are they less theological. However, because their form is more narrative, they make a more direct appeal to the imagination of the community: they appeal to that basic human instinct to be rooted and renewed by story.

STORY SECURES THE IMPORTANCE OF HISTORY AND PLACE

One of the important features of the Jewish-Christian use of story is that it affirms history and place. Some religious stories take place entirely outside of history, or they touch history only to light it with sacred flame. The Navajo have wonderful stories about the "holy people" who lived in another world and came up into this world through a reed. Ancient myths often speak of this world only to describe how, under the influence of the gods and other archetypal figures, it got to be as it is. (The story of Noah and the rainbow is, perhaps, a biblical example of this pattern.) But the mainstream of biblical stories is about the liberation of slaves and the return of exiles and the vocation of the followers of one who embraced outcasts and spoke words of forgiveness to those whom no one else would forgive and who died for his friends. It is the story told by his followers that he had "gone before them into Galilee,"[23] and of their commitment to the continuation and spread of his gospel.

THE STORY CONTINUES

We tell this story over and over again so that the story may become part of us and we may become part of the story, *because the story is not over.* The story does not belong to sacred time and sacred space: it belongs to every place where it is told and where it releases liberating power.

This ongoing *continuum* of the gospel story, with the implication that the ministry and teaching of Jesus is continued to the present day in the lives of his followers, is inferred in the biblical narrative itself. Evidence suggests that Mark's gospel originally ended at 16.8 with the women leaving the tomb in fear and amazement but with the injunction of the messenger ringing in their ears: "Go, tell his disciples and Peter that he is going ahead of you to Galilee." Jesus goes before his followers to lead them in the completion of the work he has begun. A similar message appears in Matthew's gospel, to which other material seems to have been added.

It is probable that John's gospel also originally ended earlier than the text we have received—at 20.31, immediately after Thomas's confession of faith-in-doubt, with the author's statement that his book had been written so that his readers would come to believe that Jesus is the Messiah and would thereby "have life." John's conclusion is, perhaps, more subtle, but it builds on the earlier prayer of Jesus, "As you have sent me into the world, so I have sent them into the world." The story continues with them.

It is Luke who brings to its most exalted level the vision of the continuity of our story with the biblical story. Luke wrote

---

[23] Mark 16.7

two books, a life of Jesus and a life of the apostolic church. The agenda of his books is contained in words from the Isaiah scroll which Jesus read in the synagogue at Nazareth, "The Spirit of the Lord is upon me, because he has anointed me, to bring good news to the poor. He has sent me to proclaim release to the captives and recovery of sight to the blind, to let the oppressed go free, to proclaim the year of the Lord's favour" (4.18–9).

The rest of Luke's first book (which we know as the gospel according to Luke) is his description of how this agenda was worked out in the life of Jesus. And the burden of his second book (which we know as the Acts of the Apostles) was how this agenda was worked out in the life of the Christian community.

Luke was one of the great literary craftsmen of the Bible, and we might expect him to bring his skill and talent to bear on the form of his work. Yet, one of the odd things about his second book (Acts) is that it has no satisfactory ending. Luke simply reports that Paul lived in Rome and proclaimed the kingdom of God and taught about Jesus with boldness and without hindrance—and then the book fizzles out. Or does it? I think Luke is telling his readers that the story of the second book (which is also the story of the first book) is still going on.

SOME PRACTICAL CONSIDERATIONS

The liturgy of the word is a time for sensing, whether this is fostered on a modest scale in clear, prepared, projected reading, or on a larger scale involving a dialogue reading of the gospel or a dramatic presentation. The sermon may curve that sensing experience back into the realms of thought, feeling, or intuition, but people attending the liturgy of the word should know that they have been present at the telling of the community's story, a story that *defines* the community. This sensing dimension includes even the epistles, for they too are often passionate responses to the tense situations in which early Christians found themselves, whether we are reading Paul's reaction to the Galatians' temptation to return to a ritualistic understanding of law, or his wrestling with the Corinthian church's division over both sexual scandal and charismatic worship. These stories too are not over.

FOR DISCUSSION

Read the story of Isaac and Rebekah in Genesis 24. At one level it is about racial purity—Rebekah is related to Isaac closely enough not to be a foreigner, and far enough not to make the marriage incestuous. But at another level, it is a story filled with emotion and tenderness. What do you see in relationships today that throws light *backwards* on this story? Try to retell the story so that it might affirm and strengthen relationships today.

Israel, wait for the morning

1 Is - ra - el
wait for the morn - ing, Is - ra - el
hope for the day! Though the night's
black as our hearts can re - mem - ber, O Is - ra - el
search for the way. 2 Thou who art
both rock and ref - uge, a strong-hold to
keep the land safe, come quick - ly to
heal, come quick-ly to judge, so
jus - tice and love mark our shape!

3 From dark - ness,
God shaped the light, rolled the
cha - os a - way; from the rocks and the
sands, our Gen - es - is stands, in a gar - den of
life, hope, and play.
4 From Phar - oahs to
slav - ing for bread, to jour - neys of
prom - ise a - head, in the wa - ters of
part - ing, a na - tion was start - ing to
take shape wher - ev - er God led!   To sign %S for st. 5

5 From strug - gles of
pro - phets and kings, to the dark night songs
in the strange land, in the free - ing of
cap - tives, God's free - dom song lives, in
tunes that new hearts un - der - stand!

Text: Ian Macdonald.
Music: Jim Uhrich.
Text and music © The Common Cup Company.

Mary laid her baby down

1 All the stars like spark-ling
2 To the ci - ty tem - ple
3 See the child now tall and

stones, all the bright-est an - gel songs, cir-cled
grounds, Ma-ry came with in - fant son, and she
strong, leave be-hind his boy-hood home; as he

'round a bed in a sim - ple shed, where she
ten - dered there all her warm - est prayer, as she
left that day, Ma-ry's heart gave way, and she

laid her ba - by down; and she laid her ba - by
laid her ba - by down; and she laid her ba - by
laid her ba - by down. And she laid her ba - by

down, Ma - ry laid her ba - by down; with a
down, Ma - ry laid her ba - by down; and her
down, Ma - ry laid her ba - by down; though it

lul - la - by for his new - born cry, she
songs of praise filled the ho - ly place, as she
grieved her so, still she let him go, and she

laid her ba - by down.
laid her ba - by down.
laid her ba - by down.

4 Came a

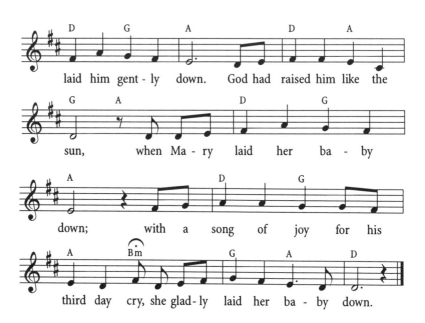

laid him gent - ly down. God had raised him like the

sun, when Ma - ry laid her ba - by

down; with a song of joy for his

third day cry, she glad - ly laid her ba - by down.

Text and music: Gordon Light. © *The Common Cup Company.*

Cry Alleluia

1 Deep in the dark earth,
2 The pow - ers are strong that hold

si - lent as night,
heart, flesh, and bone.

si - lent as death,
Si - lent to - mor - rows,

si - lent as stone,
si - lent the tears,

si - lent as breath when it's gone. Lies a
si - lent the sor - rows of years.

seed of such worth,
Seed in dark ground make

hid - den from sight, it
scarce - ly a sound, but

stirs in the dark,
lis - ten—their cry

scarce - ly a sound but the
is form - ing on wind,

beat of a heart true and strong. And a voice shall cry: al - le -
bear - ing the shape of life's dream. And a peo - ple shall cry: al - le -

lu - ia! The earth can - not hold such a life from the
lu - ia! Let com - pas - sion give hope and heart in the

sun. Give voice to the song: al - le - lu - ia! From the
night. Our love be the song: al - le - lu - ia! That

sha - dows of night comes the birth of the dawn.
calls forth the seed giv - ing birth to new life.

Text: Gordon Light and Barbara Liotscos.
Music: Gordon Light.
Text and music © The Common Cup Company.

PRAYERS OF THE PEOPLE

Most of the churches of the Reformation expressed their theological positions in statements known as "confessions," like the Augsburg Confession (1530), the Westminster Confession (1643), and other similar documents.[24] These statements are fuller than creeds, but less detailed than the great collections of closely argued compendia in which medieval theologians outlined their positions. The confessions gave the followers of a new direction a framework in which to find and maintain their position.

There is good reason to believe that the Anglican reformers intended to provide their followers with a similar doctrinal structure. The Thirty-Nine Articles were, I believe, intended to be an Anglican confession. And there is no doubt that they gave, and continue to give, an intimate profile of the Anglican reformation, an outline of the elements of tradition that are to be retained, as well as the departures from late medieval practice that are to be embraced.

There is also evidence that the Thirty-Nine Articles are a document founded on compromise, attempting to make it possible for Calvinist puritans and more traditional "high churchmen" (as they came to be called) to live in the same house, if not with comfort at least with courtesy (or perhaps if not with courtesy, at least with safety). At any rate, although

---

[24] The post-medieval Roman Catholic church, equally a product of its time although defined by opposition to Reformation principles rather than by their adoption, expressed its theological position in the Catechism of Pius V (1568), a confessional document reflecting positions adopted by the Council of Trent (1545–1563).

English law required clergy to take an oath in relation to the Articles at ordination and induction, and members of the universities to take similar oaths at certain points in their career, the Church of England *in practice* never really accepted the Articles with the heartfelt enthusiasm that stricter Protestants accorded their confessions. By the 1620s, Archbishop Bramhall could write that no one was required to believe the Articles; they were only required not to teach otherwise.

THE BOOK OF COMMON PRAYER
AS THE ANGLICAN CONFESSION

It is my own opinion that *in practice* Anglicans turned by an unlegislated agreement or consensus to the *Book of Common Prayer* as their basis of doctrine, and that the Prayer Book, reinforced somewhat by the Articles, functioned as a theological compass to Anglicans as they made their way on hitherto uncharted waters. If you wanted to know the position of the church on some subject, you started by looking up references to that subject in the Prayer Book.[25] This was, I believe, an admirable method. First, it avoided any tendency to a nit-picking interpretation of confessional statements. Second, it built itself on the beautiful notion that doctrine is primarily a matter of worship rather than a matter of classroom study. Third, it retained a sort of holy fuzziness in the area of orthodoxy, recognizing that "right belief" is a matter of the general direction in which you are going rather than the absolute precision of where you are

---

[25] To this day I would respond to a request for the Anglican "position" on any theological subject by examining first its treatment in the various prayer books—1549 as well as 1662, and other provincial variants like the Canadian books of 1922 and 1962. Second, I would see what the XXXIX Articles said on the subject. Only after determining the anchor point of the tradition would I explore treatment of the subject in subsequent Anglican history, in writings of theological opinion, theological commission reports, modern liturgical texts, Lambeth Conference and other reports, and synodical decisions, and current contextual explorations.

standing. This gave to Anglicanism its somewhat open character, ridiculed by some but valued immensely by others. This openness was not substantially affected by the creation of two distinct Prayer Book traditions in the publication of the Scottish Prayer Book of 1637, because the drift (the direction) of the two traditions was sufficiently similar to avoid occasion of alarm, in spite of significant differences. However, the development in our century of a whole collection of alternative rites has thrown the "common law" settlement of Anglican theology based on a Prayer Book foundation into some disarray. Anglicans are asking what will hold the Communion together, especially at the level of doctrine, if the Prayer Book tradition is replaced by other liturgical patterns.

UNITY BASED ON STRUCTURE

What has emerged in recent years is a growing consensus that Anglican identity and conformity will in the future be found not in the verbal similarities of rites from one Anglican province to another but in their underlying structural similarity. The Fifth International Anglican Liturgical Consultation in Dublin (1995) included among its "Principles and Recommendations" the following statement.

> In the future, Anglican unity will find its liturgical expression not so much in uniform texts as in a common approach to eucharistic celebration and a structure which will ensure a balance of word, prayer, and sacrament, and which bears witness to the catholic calling of the Anglican communion.[26]

There is an assumption behind this principle that the details of liturgy are built on a structural foundation, which is itself a deposit of common ground and which itself has theological implications. The way we do things, the sequence of events, is

---

[26] David R. Holeton, ed., *Renewing the Anglican Eucharist: Findings of the Fifth International Anglican Liturgical Consultation, Dublin, Eire, 1995,* Grove Books Limited, Cambridge, England, p. 7.

itself pregnant with meaning. As we noted in relation to the gathering rite, the accretion of new practices and the unconsidered deletion of old ones has an impact on the meaning of the event. The purpose of the study of the history of liturgy is not to rediscover and impose a "pure form" (as if such ever existed) but to understand the dynamics of what we do so that our actions may match our intent.

PRAYERS OF THE PEOPLE AS EXAMPLE OF STRUCTURE

The prayers of the people provide a case study in structure. As noted above, Justin, writing his *Apology* in Rome about the year 150, provides us with one of the earliest detailed descriptions of a celebration of the eucharist. After describing the gathering of the community and the reading of the gospel stories (what he calls, "the memoirs of the Apostles") and prophets, he continues,

> Then the reader ceases, and the president speaks, admonishing us and exhorting us to imitate these excellent examples. Then we arise all together and offer prayers; and, as we said before, when we have concluded our prayers, bread is brought, and wine and water ...[27]

Earlier Justin describes a baptism,

> After thus washing him who has been persuaded and has given his assent, we bring him to those that are called the brethren, where they are assembled, to offer prayers in common both for ourselves and for him who has been illuminated and for all men everywhere, with all our hearts, that as we have learned the truth so we may also be counted worthy to be found good citizens and guardians of the commandments, that we may be saved with an eternal salvation. We salute one another with a kiss when we have ended the prayers.[28]

---

[27] From H. Bettenson, *Documents of the Christian Church*, Oxford University Press, New York, 1947, p. 94 (Apology I.IXVII).
[28] Ibid., p. 93 (IXV).

I have quoted these two passages from Justin because they make clear a number of things about the prayers in Justin's community. The prayers were a major element in the liturgy, apparently not less important than the reading of scripture that preceded them and the table liturgy that followed them; they were offered *in common*; and their subject matter was the church and the world.

Justin is quite aware of the roles of liturgical leaders: the reader has his function, and the president of the assembly both preaches and offers the eucharistic prayer. But there is no explicit statement that the offering of the prayers is performed by an officer of the community on behalf of the rest. "Then we arise all together and offer prayers," says Justin, and, "the brethren ... offer prayers in common." And this sense of *common* prayer, as distinct from prayer offered by a leader on behalf of the people, continues to be attached to the prayers for some time, even when the form of prayers becomes a litany or dialogue involving both a leader and the congregation. According to Jungmann, Cyprian refers to the prayer as *Communis oratio*, and a number of Augustine's sermons end with the words, *Conversi ad Dominum*, calling for the congregation to turn together to the east for the intercessions.[29]

In the course of time, two things happened to the prayers of the community for the world and for themselves. First, they were clericalized, and second, they were dislocated from their place in the structure of the rite. There is some evidence that the earliest formalized shape of the intercessory prayer in Rome was a dialogue between president and people, to which the role of the deacon was gradually added.[30] An example of this form appears in the Good Friday liturgy in the *Book of Alternative*

---

[29] Jungmann, op. cit., vol. 1, p. 480f.

[30] See Jungmann, op. cit., p. 481, "In the beginning this prayer was antiphonally recited by celebrant and congregation, a practice that remained in the Roman liturgy and partly in the Egyptian. The bishop led, by first inviting to prayer; then recited his own portion and the congregation answered. Then as time went on, the deacon, who at first only announced short directions, began to take a more prominent place in most liturgies. By the end of the fourth century he took over the invitation to prayer ...."

Services, where unfortunately the role of the people has been reduced to periods of silence and the intermittent response, "Amen."[31]

In the East the role of leading intercessory prayer was taken over almost entirely by the deacon (except for a concluding collect recited by the priest). This is often explained on the pastoral ground that the deacon was responsible for visiting the sick and therefore knew who should be included in the prayers. Again unfortunately, the office of deacon, which had originally been something between a lay reader and a sexton, was increasingly clericalized, and in spite of the choir's repeated intervention *Lord, have mercy*, the prayer became something recited on behalf of the people rather than by the people.

At the same time another dynamic was working in some parts of the Christian world to move the prayers to other parts of the liturgy. In the East, intercessory prayer sprang up all over the liturgy, the opening litany at the very beginning of the public liturgy covering almost all necessary ground.[32] This had the effect of eclipsing the importance of the traditional intercession after the sermon. In the West, the prayer after the sermon disappeared entirely by the sixth century, except for the presider's invitation, "Let us pray," after which nothing of the kind was done. This bizarre arrangement remained in the Roman rite until the 1960s. (It is noteworthy that the impulse to formal intercession by the people after the sermon did not die easily and that popular forms, involving the recitation of the Lord's Prayer and Hail Mary by the people, appeared in various parts of Europe from about the 11th century on.) The bulk of intercessory prayer in the Western rite was transferred to the eucharistic prayer itself, where it was recited by the presider alone.[33]

---

[31] Another example of this form of prayer on pp. 123–126 in the *Book of Alternative Services* does suggest that the people offer their own prayers, either "silently or aloud," but there is no further rubrical provision for their involvement.

[32] It appears almost exactly reproduced as the first litany in the intercessions in the *Book of Alternative Services*.

[33] The sixth eucharistic prayer in the *Book of Alternative Services* provides an example of this.

PRAYER BOOK AND LITURGICAL MOVEMENT

The intercessory prayer was restored to the Prayer Book eucharist by Cranmer, but with no challenge to the clericalism that had overtaken it. The prayer for, "The Whole State of Christ's Church Militant Here on Earth," is a long, unvarying monologue by the priest, in which the people's only moment of participation is the final *Amen*. Further, it reflects a very settled and unprophetic view of human society, whether viewed as church or state. The model of society is pyramidal, with the monarch at the top and governors and rulers below; justice is to be administered "indifferently" (in later versions, "impartially") to the maintenance of true religion and virtue; the quality of Christian life is described in terms of "meek heart" and "due reverence," and so on. The goal is social stability, and the role of the church is to guarantee it.

One of the effects of the liturgical movement in this century has been the restoration of a more flexible form of intercessory prayer to the liturgy, with greater sensitivity to the events and concerns of the day. This process is still being assimilated in practice. Justin's ideal of common prayer is not realized when a lay person recites a monologue as tediously as priests have done, nor by the reading of litanies intended only as models and resources without adaptation to the current context. The intercessions will, I believe, die again if we do not use them as an opportunity for freshness and vitality.

THE PRAYERS AS AN INDEPENDENT ELEMENT IN THE RITE

When I first started to study liturgy, it was common to divide the rite into two parts, word and sacrament, with some sub-divisions within them. The liturgy of the word, for instance, consisted of readings, intervening psalms or other chants, sermon, possibly a profession of faith, and the prayers. Later I came to realize that the opening and closing rites also have great structural and theological significance, and I began to divide the whole event into four parts. Now I have come to realize that the prayers are a distinct element in the liturgy on their own, the third act of five in the liturgical drama. The working group assigned the task of exploring the structure of the eucharist at the 1995 Dublin Consultation has reinforced this notion.

> The intercessions, which follow the proclamation, are not merely a response to the ministry of the word, but are an essential aspect of the priestly service of the Body of Christ. Leadership of the prayers is a responsibility of members of the community other than the presider. A variety of forms may be used so that the congregation clearly participates by litany, extempore prayers, or in some other way. Prayers are normally to be offered for the world and the created order, the church and its mission, the local community and all in need.[34]

INTERCESSION AS THE PRIESTHOOD OF CHRIST

We must examine more closely what it means to say that the prayers are "an essential aspect of the priestly service of the Body of Christ." The word *priest* is confusing in English because it has two meanings. First, it is a translation of the Latin *sacerdotus* and Greek *hiereus*, denoting a person who exercises a sacred role on behalf of a community, such as one who offers sacrifice. Second, it is a corruption of the Greek word *presbyteros*, meaning elder or senator. It is also a corruption of the Greek word *presbyteros*, meaning *elder* or *senator*.

The distinction between these two meanings of *priest* is often blurred. In general, we use the word *priest* as it is based on the root-word *presbyter* to refer to the ordained ministry because the presbyters, under the bishop, were the original elders or senators, or executive committee if you like, of the church; and we use the word *priest* as it translates the Latin and Greek words *sacerdotus* and *hiereus* for the priesthood of Christ.[35] The author of

---

[34] David R. Holeton, ed., op. cit., p. 24.
[35] It is true the bishop is sometimes called *high priest* in some Christian literature but in biblical usage *hiereus*, *archiereus*, and related words refer to Christ and the community of Christ, except when a writer is speaking of Jewish or pagan figures.

the second letter of Peter uses this second root form of the word to tell his readers that they are, "a holy priesthood, to offer spiritual sacrifices acceptable to God," and "a royal priesthood."[36] It is in this sense that the offering of prayers of intercession is "an essential aspect of the priestly service of the Body of Christ": to pray for others is to participate actively in the priesthood of Christ.

One of the Latin words for *priest* in this hieratic meaning of the word is *pontifex*, which means *bridge-maker*. It is a word still used of the Pope, especially in the form *pontiff*. A priest as pontiff is one who makes a bridge between this world and another more sacred world, between the realm of mortals and the realm of the gods. I believe there is growing reason to ask if early Christians ever intended the word *priest* to carry this meaning. I wonder if the word was used ironically, even for Jesus as the Christ, against the flow of religious assumptions. In a world in which priests were powerful figures, this powerless man who lost his life in an apparently hopeless gesture on behalf of the subjugated, impoverished, and marginalized was the *true* priest. In a world in which building bridges between this world and a sacred world counted for everything, this man's priesthood (and his sacrifice of himself) collapsed the wall between them, revealing, exposing, and redeeming the sacred quality that is embedded in ordinary life.[37]

Priest as *pontifex* would involve standing *between* those for whom one prays and the remote and disconnected God who can save them, as a bridge stands between two banks of a river. *Priest* in a more radical Christian sense of the word would mean standing *with* those for whom one prays, in a totally unsentimental sense of *compassion* as *suffering with* (as Jesus did). It is in standing with others in their distress that we invoke the God who stands with suffering humanity. And this I believe is the true meaning of

---

[36] I Peter 2.4 and 9.

[37] The ironic dimensions of Christian symbolism and metaphor are more fully explored in the final chapter of this book.

intercession for Christians, not to persuade a distant God to act in contravention of ordinary laws, but to invoke for healing and renewal the divine power that is already present.

PRACTICAL CONSIDERATIONS AND QUESTIONS FOR DISCUSSION

If the liturgy of the word provides opportunity for the activity of the sensing function in our personalities, the prayer of intercession opens the door to the expression of our feelings, not romantic feelings or sentimental feelings, but a deep and quiet sense of standing with others in their joys and sorrows. Intercession as compassion is not a substitute for engagement in personal support and social action, but it is a starting point that may focus the agenda. How do we raise this important activity to the heightened level in the liturgy where it belongs? How do we make sure that it is a common act of the people (without demanding levels of participation that shy members of the congregation might find excruciating)? How do we keep it fresh and engaged without making it histrionic? These are serious questions for liturgical planners.

FOR DISCUSSION

1. Select one of the litanies or other forms of intercession in the *Book of Alternative Services* (pp. 110–128), and re-write it to reflect the news of the day, the people with whom you share your life, and those you know who are suffering.

2. Write a litany or other form of intercession of your own, with the same concerns and people in mind.

Celtic prayer

1 Be the eye of God be - tween me and each
2 Be the power of God be - tween me and each
3 Be the tear of God be - tween me and each

eye! Be the hand of God be -
power! Be the shield of God be -
tear! Be the joy of God be -

tween me and each hand! Be the
tween me and each fear! Be the
tween me and each joy! Be the

heart of God be - tween me and each heart!
strength of God be - tween me and each foe!
soul of God be - tween me and each soul!

Bless to me the thing
Bless to me the circle
Bless to me the morning

on which my eye is fixed. Bless to me the
in which my life is lived. Bless to me the
in which my life is born. Bless to me the

thing to which my hand is giv'n.
circle in which my fear sub - sides.
mid–day in which my strength is known.

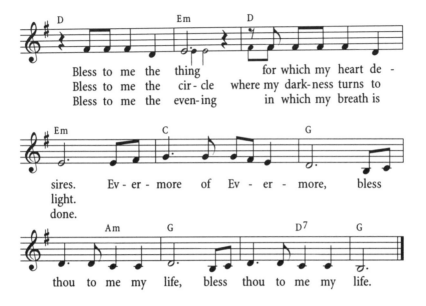

Bless to me the thing for which my heart de -
Bless to me the cir - cle where my dark-ness turns to
Bless to me the even-ing in which my breath is

sires. Ev - er - more of Ev - er - more, bless
light.
done.

thou to me my life, bless thou to me my life.

Text and music: Ian Macdonald. © *The Common Cup Company.*

So softly I'm fading

1 Come a - way, my own dear ones. So
2 Tell God's name to the wee ones. So
3 Take a - way eyes of dim - ness. So
4 Like the dream of his ris - ing and the

soft - ly I'm fad - ing, and weigh down my heart at the
soft - ly I'm fad - ing. Let Christ be the won - der and the
soft - ly I'm fad - ing. Let Christ be the guest, and the
com - ing of glo - ry, let Christ be the bond hold - ing

foot of the sea. Je - sus' blood for my
wound in all things. Je - sus' blood for my
least, and the host. Je - sus' blood for my
both you and me. Je - sus' blood for our

sor - row, his hand for my guid - ing. O, give now your
heal - ing, his tears for my break - ing. O, give now your
bind - ing. His word for my keep - ing. O, give now your
sav - ing, his bread for re - deem - ing. O, give now your

bless - ing, like the dawn - ing of day.
bless - ing, like the dawn - ing of day.
bless - ing, like the dawn - ing of day.
bless - ing, like the dawn - ing of day.

Text and music: Ian Macdonald. © *The Common Cup Company.*

THE TABLE

HISTORY AND FAITH

One of the consequences of biblical scholarship during the last two centuries has been the realization that the Bible contains and reflects some tension between history and faith. This has been a very difficult discovery for some people, and those who find it too hard often take refuge in so-called fundamentalist positions, which insist on the literal truth of every biblical statement and account. There was a Baptist minister somewhere in my childhood who was asked if he believed that Jonah was really swallowed by the whale. He is reported to have replied that if the Bible said that Jonah swallowed the whale he would believe it.

I think we have come to realize that, while Judaism and Christianity are passionately committed to their historical basis and that the Bible itself is rooted in the formative experience of the people of God in history, it is is also true that much of the Bible was written primarily to communicate and foster faith. History and faith may overlap, but they are not necessarily the same thing.

History is about the details of what happened. I remember a friend of mine at Oxford who "read" history, who reconstructed some critical events in the French Revolution on an almost hour-by-hour basis for his final examinations. Faith is different. Faith is concerned with a lifestyle based on an inner vision of the ultimate nature of things, which the experience of certain events has released and made available. It is like the difference between a photograph and an icon. A photograph tells you what the camera "saw" at a certain place and moment (in theory at least, because even cameras can be made to interpret); an icon tells you how a community has understood some event and, perhaps, what its implications are for those who contemplate it today.

I have an icon of the last supper on my dining-room wall. It shows Jesus standing behind a Russian-style altar at which the disciples are lined up to receive communion from his hands. The room is richly decorated in gold and dark red, except for one pillar, which is painted a sickly green and whose decorations form the outline of a vast and hideous face whose yawning mouth will swallow Jesus into the events of betrayal, torture, and death. The icon is not a rejection of history but rather an interpretation of history, intended to make the eternal meaning of the events available to the eye of faith.

Sometimes in the debates of the last two centuries, scholars have confidently set out to reduce the Jesus story to photographic history. At other points they have despaired of the historical challenge, concluding that we have nothing but the appeal to blind belief. Quite recently the conversation has become livelier, not least because the discovery of the Dead Sea scrolls and other literature of the period in which Jesus lived has provided new tools for the reconstruction of his context and consequently for the evaluation of biblical material that may, in fact, represent developments of thought in the community of believers considerably beyond the positions Jesus may have held. Personally, I believe questions of history and faith must go hand in hand for Christians. We have to ask both what was really going on and also what the total picture, the events and the understanding of them, means for the way we are going to live our lives.

Christians are too easily tempted by one of our most ancient heresies called *docetism* (from the Greek word *to seem*). Docetism teaches that Jesus only seemed to be human, but that his deity was the reality. Docetism is your logical conclusion if you despair of knowing or caring about the historical conditions of Jesus' life. I believe that authentic biblical Christianity must insist that Jesus is a man in and through whom we see God, and not a god masquerading as a man. And this means that we must struggle with his historical setting, however difficult that may be.

WHAT WAS JESUS DOING?

One of the leading figures in this field of endeavour, John Dominic Crossan, has attempted to determine what Jesus was actually doing, and what was the largely invisible background that provided the context for his activity and teaching.[38] Crossan explores the conditions of life of Mediterranean agricultural communities like Galilee, and the economic and political straits in which peasants in the Roman empire found themselves. And Crossan concludes that the irreducible minimum of Jesus' ministry was two-fold: he healed without price and, in a society that was economically and religiously stratified, he promoted egalitarianism, which found practical expression in common meals shared by those who otherwise could not have eaten together.[39] Both of these activities must be seen as practical expressions of his proclamation of the kingdom of God, as the way the country would be run if God were in charge and not Caesar. We can see in the gospel accounts that,

> Miracle and parable, healing and eating were calculated to force individuals into unmediated physical and spiritual contact with God, and unmediated physical and spiritual contact with

---

[38] See John Dominic Crossan, *The Historical Jesus: The Life of a Mediterranean Jewish Peasant*, Harper SanFrancisco, 1991; *Jesus: A Revolutionary Biography*, Harper SanFrancisco, 1994; *The Essential Jesus: What Jesus Really Taught*, Harper SanFrancisco, 1994; *Who Killed Jesus?*, Harper SanFrancisco, 1995.

[39] There is a similar element in Sikh liturgy. At major worship events a porridge made of wholewheat flour, crude sugar, and water is distributed before the conclusion of the rite. It was introduced by Guru Nanak, the founder of Sikhism, to guarantee that Hindu converts would abandon traditional prohibitions against members of different castes eating together. If you wanted to be a Sikh, you had to eat the *communal* porridge.

one another. He announces, in other words, the unmediated or brokerless kingdom of God.[40]

EATING AND DRINKING IN THE REIGN OF GOD

If this line of thought is correct, it becomes important for us to look at the eating and drinking aspect of the eucharist from the point of view of the whole of Jesus' ministry and not in terms of the last supper only. The roots of the eucharist are in the many meals involving Jesus and his followers, meals whose very occurrence had radical religious and political implications. The roots of the eucharist *as we know it* may also be in the many subsequent gentile Mediterranean practices (the meals of memorial societies, perhaps) that became attached to Christian practice. Once again it is important to ask the structural question: is there a pattern below the surface of what we do at the Lord's table that will illuminate our worship for us?

There are two answers to this question: yes, there are important structural patterns in the whole of what we do at the table, and there are also important structural patterns in the prayer that lies at the centre of our worship at the table.

Dom Gregory Dix looked at the words attributed to Jesus at the last supper and saw in them the shape of the liturgy.[41] The gospels say that Jesus took bread, gave thanks, broke the bread,

---

[40] Crossan, *Who Killed Jesus?*, p. 198.

[41] G. Dix, *The Shape of the Liturgy*, Dacre Press, Westminster, 1945. Dix actually notes that the biblical record indicates a seven-unit shape at the last supper, i.e., taking bread, giving thanks, breaking, giving, taking the cup, giving thanks, giving, which was collapsed into four actions involving bread and wine simultaneously before any more or less complete extant eucharistic rites appeared. Perhaps something of this transition may be seen in the various accounts of the feeding of the multitude. Mark's accuont of the feeding of the four thousand involves two acts of thanksgiving/blessing, one over bread and one over fish, and John leans in the same direction. Mark's account of the feeding of the five thousand, Matthew's two accounts, and Luke's account are, with minor discrepancies among them, very close to Dix's four-action shape.

and gave it to those at table with him. Actually, this sequence of actions also appears as a formula in the accounts of the feeding of the multitude, as well as in the story of the meal at Emmaus. Mark 6.41, for instance, reads, "*Taking* the five loaves and the two fish, he looked up to heaven, and *blessed* and *broke* the loaves, and *gave* them to his disciples to set before the people," and Luke 24.30 reads, "When he was at the table with them, he *took* bread, *blessed* and *broke* it, and *gave* it to them." Dix associated the acts of taking, blessing, breaking, and giving with the liturgical pattern of offertory, consecration, fraction, and communion.

Dix's neat scheme has been criticized by later scholars who suggest that *taking* and *breaking* were simply utilitarian actions, necessary for the completion of the ritual, and that the essential elements of the rite were blessing (giving thanks) and eating and drinking. On the other hand, there is no doubt that generations of Christians have seen a wider pattern. The preparatory provision of food and the preparation of the table may not correspond exactly with Jesus' taking of the bread and cup into his hands, but they are actions of such significance that some traditions have called the whole of the eucharist, "the offering." The "breaking of bread" was perhaps the earliest Christian name for the eucharistic rite, and it is still its primary name among some Christian groups today.[42] These are actions bursting with meaning, in spite of their practical origin.

What does it mean to set the table? Setting the table is, first of all, an act of hospitality. It is a concrete expression of generosity that, in theological and sacramental terms, mirrors and communicates the generosity of God as source of being and life. It is an act of *compassion*, not in the sense of reacting sympathetically to the pain of someone for whom we are sorry, but in the sense of *experiencing with* others, being with others, whether in pain, frustration, marginalization, or longing for wholeness (not to forget joy and pleasure). It indicates the intention to eat and drink with others. The table and the food

---

[42] Acts 2.42.

provided on it define the community like the place-cards at a banquet. This is something we are doing together.

Setting the table also secures the *sensuality* of the event: this is not to be an exercise in mental prayer or communal meditation. This event involves physical objects, produce of the earth that has been shaped by human labour, and it involves the dishes and tablecloths and napkins that are required in consuming food. There is stuff here that can be tasted and smelled, and that will go stale and bad if uncared for. The *materiality* of human experience, with all its fragile ambiguity, is honoured in the act of preparing the table.

The preparation of the table cannot be separated from the eating and drinking, which take place at the other end of the structure of eucharistic events. The "taking" and the "giving" are complementary actions. We prepare the table so that we may eat and drink; we eat and drink at the table to which we have been called. They are not cause and effect but opposite sides of the same coin. The table and everything that takes place at it determines our equal, unbrokered citizenship in the kingdom of God.

This physical sharing of material food with persons of flesh and blood runs counter to a recurring Christian temptation to spiritualize and clericalize the elements of the eucharist and to distance them from the people who form the church. We are used to a piety in which the bread and cup of the eucharist are spiritualized to the extent that they have nothing to do with ordinary bread and wine, and in which *my* communion with God utterly transcends *our* communion together. This is not new. As early as the fourth century, Theodore of Mopsuestia (ca. 350–428) described the preparation of the table by the deacons in terms of placing the dead body of the Lord on the altar as tomb, so that he might rise again by the action of the Holy Spirit in the consecration.[43] A not dissimilar atmosphere pervades aspects of the Byzantine procession of the bread and cup to the table. The

---

[43] Dix, op. cit., p. 282ff.

action is described as though it was taking place in heaven and the worshippers are depicted as angels.

In the medieval West, both preparation of the table and eating and drinking became increasingly remote from the people, in terms of physical distance and visibility because of the design of many churches, and in terms of lay involvement because of the clericalization of the rite. In some pre-modern Western rites, the actual preparation of bread and cup took place at high mass during the singing of the Gloria, and communion of the people was banished from the rite altogether. The preparation of the table was consequently remote and clerical, and the communion of the people was individual and personal (as well as rare). The sharing of food—eating bread from the same plate and drinking wine from the same cup—as an act of participation together in God's kingdom was eclipsed.

The breaking of the bread is similarly freighted with significance. From an early date Christians recognized that the breaking of one loaf into many particles carries the reverse implication that the many particles equal one loaf. It is a sign of our common life, our common vision, our common destiny. The *Didache*, a second-century Christian document, contains the breathtaking words, "As this broken bread was scattered over the mountains, and when brought together became one, so let your Church be brought together from the ends of the earth into your kingdom."[44] That says it all. Later confusion of the breaking of the bread with the mutilation of the body of Jesus on the cross (like the parallel confusion of the preparation of the table with an offering by the church, which is in some way distinct from Jesus' offering of his life for his friends) misses the sacramental point. Both the preparation of the table and the breaking of the bread are about the gathering of a community of "nobodies" into the event in which the kingdom of God is realized.

---

[44] R.C.D. Jasper and G.J. Cuming, *Prayers of the Eucharist: Early and Reformed*, Oxford University Press, New York, 1980, p. 15.

I have discussed the first, third, and fourth elements (taking, breaking, and giving) in the structure of the table liturgy. The second element, giving thanks or blessing, requires special treatment. It is a distinctive feature of Jewish worship, especially Jewish worship in a domestic setting, and it was clearly of great importance to the authors of the New Testament documents. The descriptions of the last supper, the accounts of the feeding of the multitude, the story of the supper at Emmaus—all refer to Jesus blessing or giving thanks over the food that is to be shared. Paul asks the Corinthians, "The cup of *blessing* that we bless, is it not a sharing in the blood of Christ?"[45] But what was the nature of this blessing?

We cannot be absolutely sure of the exact text of the blessing-thanksgiving prayer that Jesus used at meals with his followers, but the text of a prayer in use at that time gives us a strong hint of what the prayer he used was probably like. It consists of three parts, the first two of which are closely related. The first is the blessing of God who nourishes, and the second is a thanksgiving for the land and the combination of covenant, law, life, and food that the land represents for Jewish people. The third part is a prayer for the restoration of the people to God's purpose.

1 *Blessing of him who nourishes*
Blessed are you, Lord our God, King of the universe, for you nourish us and the whole world with goodness, grace, kindness, and mercy.
Blessed are you, Lord, for you nourish the universe.

2 *Blessing for the earth*
We will give thanks to you, Lord our God, because you have given us for our inheritance a desirable land, good

---

[45] 1 Corinthians 10.16 (my italics).

and wide, the covenant and the law, life and food.
And for all these things we give you thanks and bless your
name for ever and beyond.
Blessed are you, Lord our God, for the earth and for food.

3   *Blessing for Jerusalem*
Have mercy, Lord our God, on us your people Israel,
and your city Jerusalem, on your sanctuary and your
dwelling place, on Zion the habitation of your glory,
and the great and holy house over which your name is
invoked. Restore the kingdom of the house of David to
its place in our days, and speedily build Jerusalem ....

Blessed are you, Lord, for you build Jerusalem. Amen.[46]

Notice the structure of the prayer. It begins by blessing God for
creation, goodness, grace, kindness, and mercy. Then it continues
with thanksgiving for the land *which is the Jewish symbol of the
salvation God has given* ("The Lord brought us out of Egypt with
a mighty hand and an outstretched arm ... and he brought us into
this place and gave us this land").[47] Finally, it prays for restoration
and completion of that salvation in the future. The pattern is
thanksgiving for creation and salvation, followed by supplication.

Thomas Talley, an Anglican liturgical scholar, finds in one
major stratum of early Christian eucharistic prayers this same
pattern: praise of the Creator, thanksgiving for salvation in Christ,
and supplication for the fulfilment of God's purpose.[48] Talley
suggests that proclamation of the events of the last supper was

---

[46] Jasper and Cuming, op. cit., p. 9f. The authors say the prayer, "is thought by
scholars to be a possible ultimate source of the Christian eucharistic thanksgiving
..." and that "most of the blessing is at least contemporary with the lifetime of
Jesus." A fourth section, which I have not quoted, was added after the fall of
Jerusalem in 70 C.E.

[47] Deuteronomy 26.8f.

[48] Thomas Talley, "Eucharistic Prayers, Past, Present and Future," in *Revising
the Eucharist: Groundwork for the Anglican Communion*, ed. David R. Holeton,
Grove Books, Bramcote, Nottingham, 1994, p. 9.

attached to the prayer of thanksgiving for salvation, thus linking a particular celebration of the eucharist to the saving work of Christ. In effect, the prayer says, "we give thanks for salvation in Christ who told us to do this to remember his saving work, and we are doing it."

The supplication for the completion of God's kingdom became a prayer for the work of the Holy Spirit in the church's life, and eventually expanded into a petition that the Holy Spirit would sanctify the bread and wine to be Christ's body and blood so that his people would accomplish his will in the world.

As long as the prayer retained this Jewish shape and structure, it provided a strong definition of authentic Christian piety in terms of exclusive reliance on the Giver of all, discovery of the new world vision that Jesus gave to his followers in word and action, and prayer for the completion of God's kingdom. When, however, the supplication section of the prayer crept backwards to take over most of the prayer's agenda (as happened especially in the West), it became increasingly an expression of concern that the bread and wine would really become the body and blood of the Lord, and it led to preoccupation with the moment at which that happened.

In the second *Book of Common Prayer* (1552), Cranmer gave Anglicanism a eucharistic prayer with only a nodding reference to thanksgiving, no mention of creation, an orthodox but remote proclamation of salvation, and a central supplication, "that we, receiving these thy creatures of bread and wine, according to thy Son our Saviour Jesus Christ's holy institution, in remembrance of his death and passion, may be partakers of his most blessed body and blood." There is no mention of the God who nourishes the world with goodness, grace, kindness, and mercy, of the law of love, of the gifts of life and food, or of hope for the realization of God's reign of peace and justice made present in Christ in all the world. He seems to have fallen into the trap (described in Baumstark's principle) that when reform eventually happens and trimming takes place, *the older rather than the newer material tends to be pruned*. With the best of intentions, Cranmer produced a medieval prayer.

Jesus came proclaiming what the world would be like if God were in charge instead of Caesar. He gathered around him the "nobodies" of a peasant culture and told them, by sign and word, that they could, if they wanted, belong to this "reign of God." He ate and drank with them, across a network of forbidden barriers, proving the acceptance of the unacceptable, making acceptance of the unacceptable the ultimate condition of belonging. Together they took their places around a table, taught by him they gave thanks for creation and new being, and they prayed for the completion of God's reign. The one loaf was divided into pieces for all. And they ate and drank.

Most of us cannot recover the peasant simplicity of these events, but we must recover the meaning of their pattern. The structure of the table rite as a whole, as I have described it, will tell us who we are. The structure of the prayer should tell us what we are here for, indeed what Christian life is for—to give thanks for creation, goodness, kindness, and mercy; to proclaim the story of Jesus' revelation of a new humanity in relationship with God; and to long for the reign of God. Thus considered, the table prayer is our ultimate faith-statement, the ground upon which we open ourselves to the transforming power of grace.[49] The table is our whole spirituality.

---

[49] The prayer at the table is the true creed of the eucharistic rite, recited by the president and acclaimed by the people's, "Amen." Other creeds, originally catechumenal and later used as concise doctrinal statements, entered the eucharistic liturgy more as proofs of orthodoxy than as professions of a covenant relationship with God. A sixth-century patriarch of Jerusalem, suspected of Monophysitism, zealously ordered recitation of the creed at every celebration of the eucharist. He was copied all over the East. Later in the same century the practice spread to a region of Spain under Eastern control when a Visigoth king and his subjects renounced Arianism by reciting the Nicene Creed, the use of which was then ordered at every mass. Jungmann says that when the Emperor Henry II visited Rome in 1014 he was surprised that the creed was not sung. Roman clergy explained to him that frequent recitation of the creed was not necessary there because the Roman church had never been in error. (See Jungmann, op. cit., vol. 1, pp. 468–470.) It seems that recitation of the creed may have had more to do with keeping heresy out than with affirming the nature of belief.

FOR DISCUSSION

What would you, as a twentieth-century Christian, like the third section of the Jewish prayer over the bread to say? Begin, "Send your Holy Spirit to ... " and fill in the dots.

FIRST POSTSCRIPT: WHO MAY EAT AND DRINK?

For centuries Christian tradition has built strong walls around the Lord's table, walls of custom and discipline that limit access. For Anglicans, the discipline reflected by the Prayer Book was intended to restrict communion (eating and drinking at the table) to those who had been confirmed, that was the culminating event in a process that included instruction in the creed, the ten commandments, the Lord's Prayer, and the catechism.[50] The requirement of confirmation by the bishop has probably been observed more frequently in the last century or so than earlier, because the development of the railways and modern highway systems has made episcopal visitations more than a rare possibility. In the past, many Anglicans (perhaps most) must have availed themselves of the exception that opened communion not only to those who had received the laying-on of hands but also to those who were, "ready and willing to be confirmed." But in any case, until relatively recently no one questioned that confirmation was the *normal* gateway to communion.

The norm of confirmation as the point of entry to the table has been challenged on a number of fronts. The ecumenical movement and the pursuit of organic unity that it has fostered, have raised questions about the necessity of *episcopal* confirmation. If Anglicans unite with Christians who have hitherto enjoyed a non-episcopal form of church government, is it necessary for each of them to be *episcopally* confirmed? History suggests that those most opposed to union with "non-conformists" have tended to insist most stridently on episcopal confirmation as the "completion" of baptism.

---

[50] See, for instance, the *Book of Common Prayer* of the Anglican Church of Canada, 1962, p. 530, "Take care that he be taught the Creed, the Ten Commandments and the Lord's Prayer, and be further instructed in the Church Catechism; and then be brought to the Bishop to be confirmed by him ..."

The notion that baptism is complete in itself, and that nothing further is necessary for the participation of a believer in the Lord's table, has itself widened the field of access to communion. Western Christians have looked at Eastern practice, where children receive communion at the time of their baptism and more or less continuously for some years thereafter, and have asked increasingly why admission to one sacrament is based on the faith of the community in which the subject is being nurtured, while admission to the other requires training, memorization, intellectual comprehension, and a quasi-sacramental gesture. Scholarship has tended to reinforce this line of thought with the suggestion, now gaining support, that confirmation as it is practised in the West is the residuum of a second anointing after baptism, originally unique to Rome, and not the counterpart of a more or less universal act of anointing that, by gesture, interpreted baptism as the "Christing" (which, in Greek, is what "anointing" means) of the newly-baptized.

A natural pastoral consequence of all of this has been the opening of communion to unconfirmed young children in a growing number of provinces of the Communion (with the understanding that confirmation may be the way in which individuals identify a more personal commitment at a later point in their lives), and the raising of doubt about traditional rigidity elsewhere. But even this considerable development in discipline, a surprise in many traditional quarters, is based on the continuation of an inflexible relationship between baptism and the table, and the assumption that the former is the invariable prelude to the latter.

The inflexibility of this relationship may no longer be assumed and is, indeed, questioned on two fronts. On the most basic level, there are those who ask how and why we should fence the table of the Lord when it appears that the very essence of Jesus' ministry involved almost indiscriminate eating and drinking across the fixed lines of social and religious conduct. If Jesus ate and drank with "sinners" (the impure and unworthy), apparently without reference to their status within his movement, can we turn away those who may see the gleam of the kingdom's light through a chance encounter with our eucharistic assembly?

This argument must be taken seriously. The line of tension that separates it from a more "orthodox" tradition may run right through the New Testament itself. There are two versions of the parable of a great banquet at which those who were invited but did not come were replaced by "outsiders" recruited from the streets (Matthew 22.1–14 and Luke 14.15–24). The endings of the two versions are, however, quite different. Luke emphasizes the assembly of a motley crowd composed of "the poor, the crippled, the blind, and the lame," and others who could be gathered from the roads and lanes. In Matthew's version, the host (a king) goes to see his guests (both bad and good) and finds a man without a wedding robe, who is consequently thrown into outer darkness. Is it possible that Luke's account reflects the "open table" approach of Jesus (who was castigated for eating and drinking with outcasts and sinners), while Matthew reflects the more cautious approach of the church as an emerging institution, and insists on the wedding robe of baptism as a condition of entry to the table? (It is noteworthy that John's account of the last supper begins with the water-rite of footwashing, which cannot help but suggest baptismal overtones and which survived as an element of the Ambrosian baptismal rite into the middle of this century.)

The relationship of baptism and the eucharist may be defended on the grounds of antiquity and the biblical record. In addition, the dual pattern of birth and nourishment, washing and table, which echoes and builds on the life process itself, lends its profound appeal. From the point of view of the Christian community, baptism is the threshold sacrament, the event that brings together the double crises of the Lord's self-giving and the new follower's intention of commitment. And yet, the very fact of the open table as the paradigm of Jesus' proclamation of good news warns us against a legalism that might quench a smoking flax or break a bruised reed. In terms of theological order, baptism must, perhaps, precede the table; in the face of pastoral challenge and care for those in spiritual need, theological order may have to bend. Today I regret the assiduity with which I once protected holy things, which need no protector but God.

But the issue does not rest on this pastoral level alone, and may also be pursued in current theories related to both the status and dignity of baptism and the quality of Christian discipline. There is no doubt that, from the time Christianity became a legal religion early in the fourth century, baptism gradually degenerated from a crisis rite implying risky commitment to a sign of belonging in a general way to an increasingly nominal Christian culture. Eventually *real* commitment had to find expression in *extraordinary* forms of devotion, such as becoming a hermit or joining a monastic community or (later) going on pilgrimage or on a crusade. The "mainline" churches of the twentieth century (whether Protestant or Catholic) inherited, for the most part, an institutional and technical approach to baptism and membership in the Christian community. "Joining the church" or "going into the church" became a term that referred to ordination rather than baptism.

Twentieth-century reformers have sometimes tried to rekindle dormant corporate zeal by imposing what they perceive to be the baptismal discipline of old. In the Roman Catholic church, this has taken the form of the Rite for the Christian Initiation of Adults, which involves an elaborate process of instructive preparation divided into stages that are interspersed by liturgical events and coordinated with the liturgical year. A very positive dimension of the RCIA (as this process is known) is the involvement of lay members of the congregation as sponsors, not only in a formal sense but also as fellow-pilgrims with those who are moving towards baptism.

Not a few Anglicans look wistfully at the RCIA as a means of restoring the integrity of the baptismal rite and its identification with committed rather than nominal membership, and some provinces have acted to adopt similar processes. Others (this writer included) recognize the need for a systematic and congregationally-oriented method of preparation for baptism but question the rigidity of the proposed framework—the presupposition that models that failed the church in the fourth and fifth centuries are likely to succeed today simply because they are old, and the apparent assumption in the minds of some supporters of the process that there is one way to be or become Christian and that they know what it is.

Baptism in the New Testament seems to have been a spontaneous, almost charismatic, response to the gospel's new vision of a world of reversed values. Once the Ethopian eunuch had grasped the meaning of the role of Jesus as the Messiah, he said to Philip the deacon, "Here is water—why can't I be baptized?" Later in Acts we read that, when Peter had proclaimed the gospel in the house of Cornelius and those who heard him had responded positively, "Peter said, 'Can anyone withhold the water for baptizing these people who have received the Holy Spirit just as we have?' So he ordered them to be baptized in the name of Jesus Christ." Sometimes the prolonged stages and intermittent ceremonies of the catechumenal process, tied as they are to the cycle of the liturgical year and its seasons, seem to owe more to the ancient pagan mystery religions that Christianity was replacing than to evangelical inspiration.

But the problem goes deeper. Richard Fabian has argued beautifully that in the teaching and example of Jesus the acceptance of those whom others consider unacceptable is central. On this ground he describes the practice of the church he serves:

> We welcome all to share the eucharist without qualification or exception. Once people have there experienced God's unconditional grace and acceptance, we invite them to commit themselves to Christ's ministry of service to the world. We baptize them into this ministry, if they are not already baptized, and enroll them in our work ...[51]

---

[51] Richard Fabian, "Patterning the sacrament after Christ," in *Open: Journal of the Associated Parishes for Liturgy and Mission*, Fall 1994, vol. 40, no. 3, p. 1.

Fabian avoids any suggestion that the church community would, by this discipline, be divided into a "common" membership of unbaptized communicants and a "preferred" membership of those who have been fully initiated. But one has to wonder if that would happen if his proposal were to move from the tight atmosphere of a small and specialized congregation (St. Gregory Nyssen Episcopal Church in San Francisco) into the wider and more casual circles of the church. This possibility has not escaped those with a more rigorous approach. Maggie Ross, writing several years ago as an Anglican solitary living at Christ Church Cathedral, Oxford, proposed communion of the unbaptized within a framework in which, "Baptism would be reserved for those who live a conscious commitment to the kenotic, eucharistic ungraspingness of Christ's priestly humility in every facet of life." [52]

Ross suggests,

> In adult education for baptism, the mere intellectual qualification of the catechumen would be the least consideration. Baptism should be the sign of a deep experiential understanding of and commitment to a kenotic life, what it means to be willing to look at God gaze on Gaze. It would mean a serious confrontation with the fear of death. Some few people might be ready for and desirous of baptism early on, even as preadolescents; others might reach this passage only on their deathbeds. Some might never be ready.[53]

In short, baptism is for an elite.

It seems to this writer that, if we take nothing else from the gospel, it should be the realization that there is no room in the movement established by Jesus of Nazareth for an elite. James and John asked for an elite status in the kingdom and they were told that those who would be first must be servants of all. When Paul faced the elitism of the charismatic members of the

---

[52] Maggie Ross, *Pillars of Flame*, Harper and Row, San Francisco, 1988, p. 177.
[53] Ibid., p. 179.

Corinthian congregation, he wrote to tell them that neither prophecy, tongues, nor knowledge had any staying power; they would all end, and only self-giving love would remain.

We are used to the self-caricature of those whose genuine desire for holiness becomes an affectation that others dismiss as "holier than thou." The same dynamic applies to all other standards of elitism, even the reverse elitism of humility and self-abasement. We bring nothing to our participation in the Christian movement but the image of God in which we have been made, and our brokenness—and we can congratulate ourselves for neither. Every symbolic dimension of baptism is anti-elitist: baptism is a matter of returning to the primordial waters of creation and birth in order to start again in the kingdom community in which there is, by definition, no elite.

One of our problems in dealing with any sacramental discipline is the prevailing assumption that the sacraments belong to the church, which somehow "owns" them. Nothing could be further from the truth. Only a church that has lost sight of itself as *movement* and stumbled into the role of *institution* could make that mistake. (The movement needs some institutional structure, but it does not exist for the structure.) Baptism and the eucharist, as the outward and visible signs of the Christ who is the outward and visible sign of God, precede the church. The church is their witness, their banner-bearer, their steward, not their reliquary or prison. The question is not how to ration out the sacraments in remedial doses but how to call people to discover the saving power they represent and evoke.

Certainly we must move away from a mechanical and even superstitious practice of baptism as the technical initiation of a child into a Christendom culture that no longer exists. But we do not achieve that worthy goal by the imposition of regulations on people who do not understand them. Casual visitors are not a nuisance, and nominal Christians are not a sign of decadence. Both groups challenge us to present them with a vision of the world made new in the likeness of God's reign. The proponents of the communion of all those who are sufficiently attracted by that vision to stretch out their hands at the Lord's table are right, in so far as they reflect this principle. But they are wrong if they raise high walls of baptismal discipline to create a new standard of elitism.

While I prefer to keep as normal the traditional pattern of washing before eating (bath before table) within a framework of reasonable tolerance, I believe we must make them both very accessible. The challenge is not to shift from an easy discipline to a hard one, but to shift from an easy discipline based on social conformity to an open practice based on the attractive and arresting power of the good news. Both baptism and the Lord's table must be open and available to those who find themselves attracted, however spontaneously and suddenly, to follow Jesus Christ into a community in which the ordinary values of power and domination are reversed, in which freedom may be found, in which the lines of demarcation of race, colour, social class, and ritual purity are erased—a community that witnesses to God as the power of personal and social salvation.

> "It is I, Jesus, who sent my angel to you with this
> testimony for the churches. I am the root and the
> descendant of David, the bright morning star."
> The Spirit and the bride say, "Come."
> And let everyone who hears say, "Come."
> And let everyone who is thirsty come.
> Let *anyone who wishes* take the water of life as a gift.[54]

---

[54] Revelation 22.16–17 (italics mine).

Invitation

live to share its toll.   Have we   had e-nough of

cross - es,   or dy-ing to our   dreams?

Life is full   and mov - ing,   bul - ging at the seams.

Yet the   cup   is   al - ways spill-ing,   love pro -

vid - ed   for   our   will-ing,   drink deep when you are

rea-dy,   be   filled with ho - ly   dreams. Yet the cup is   al-ways

spill-ing love   pro - vid - ed   for   our   will-ing,   drink

deep when you are   rea-dy,   be   filled with ho - ly   dreams.

Text and music: Gordon Light. © *The Common Cup Company.*

Till you come

1 We will still   break the   bread   till you
2 We will still   seek   your   peace   till you
3 We will still   dream your   dreams   till you
4 We will still   be   your   song   till you
5 We will still   claim your   Spir-it   till you

come.   We will still   lift the   cup,   'though our
come.   We will still   live your love   from our
come.   We will still   lift the   prayers,   that our
come.   We will still   find the   joy   in your
come.   We will still   feel the   fire   of your

hands shake with   their   tremb - ling.
birth - cry to   our   end - ing.
hearts and   lips   are   mend - ing.
call - ing   and   your   send - ing.
pres - ence nev - er   end - ing.

Text and music: Ian Macdonald. © *The Common Cup Company.*

UNGATHERING

THE ROLE OF RELIGION

Some years ago the English novelist and essayist A.N. Wilson wrote a little book in which he argued that religion, in spite of its positive aspects, has been the occasion of so many human evils that we ought to give it up.[55] When we look at the role of religious identity in Ireland (to name but one Christian example), and the global reinforcement of prejudice of all kinds in the name of God, we may see some validity in his argument. It does, however, miss the point. It is rather like saying that there is a lot of rape about so everyone should give up sex, or there is a lot of obesity around so everyone should give up eating. Religion isn't going to go away (although its forms of expression may change) because religion is fundamentally the expression of a basic human drive, the drive to order the realm of experience, inner and outer, through the use of symbol, ritual, and story. Religion may

---

[55] A.N. Wilson, *Against Religion*, Chatto Counterblasts, No. 19, Chatto and Windus, 1991. Wilson says, "Religion is the tragedy of mankind. It appeals to all that is noblest, purest, loftiest in the human spirit, and yet there scarcely exists a religion which has not been responsible for wars, tyrannies and the suppression of the truth" (p. 1). Later he states, "The general majority of religious people are ... drawn to the organized religions of the world by the same impulses which move all human beings when confronting the mystery of things—in landscape, in music, in the experiences of love and loss. They do not join these religions, or remain in the religion of their parents, primarily because they believe the fantastical claims and doctrines, but because they believe in the ideals, and they believe that all these good things will be lost unless, like frightened children, they hold on to the ugly and evil things in their religion for fear of losing what they love. It is one of the most depressing features of the religious psyche that in time it comes positively to love the authoritarianism and spiritual bullying and intolerance and sheer bare-faced is dishonesty which characterizes the major world religions" (p. 47).

develop into much more than this, but this is where it begins, this is its primary sphere of operation.

SACRED AND PROFANE

Religion orders first of all the distinction between sacred and profane, dividing space into ordinary space and sacred space, and time into ordinary time and sacred time.[56] There is the realm of sacred power, of the gods if you like, and there is the ordinary realm of passing human life. On a festival, especially the new year, or in a certain cave, or under a certain tree, you may pass briefly from one realm to the other, renewing and reinvigorating your ordinary life. Telling the story of the sacred origins of your people not only reminds you of who you are but also recapitulates your origin, renewing you in that creative power. These are the building blocks of human religious experience. The great religions collect them together and provide them with a framework. In a secular society, where such systems are rejected, these basic elements of religion may reappear in truncated and usually harmless forms, like loyalty to certain athletic teams and television serials, or in more sinister forms such as nationalism (my country is sacred, other countries are not), and racism (my people are authentic humanity and our blood should not be mixed with that of lesser beings).

FIRST RELIGION AND SECOND RELIGION

We may label religion as I have sketched it, "First Religion." There is, however, a counterforce working in the religious sphere of human experience that attempts to use the same building blocks in another way. I will call this counterforce, "Second

---

[56] See Mircea Eliade, *The Sacred and the Profane*, Harcourt, Brace and Company, Inc., 1959.

Religion."[57] First Religion sets this world in tension with another realm or world of being, from which power may be invoked. Second Religion seeks to find the sacred, the creative and regenerative centre, in the experience of life itself.

The Exodus story is a wonderful step into Second Religion because it represents the discovery of God as the power of salvation in the process of human history. The prophets, especially Amos and Micah, develop this theme. According to them, God is not interested in festivals and sacrifices that build a fleeting bridge between this world and the sacred realm: God wants justice, righteousness, kindness, and humility.[58] This is where the sacred is to be found. The author of Isaiah 58 addresses those who wonder why their First Religion isn't working, why their fervent fasting does not result in God's intervention in their national program. God, through the prophet, answers in terms of Second Religion.

> Is not this the fast that I choose: to loose the bonds of injustice, to undo the thongs of the yoke, to let the oppressed go free, and to break every yoke? Is it not to share your bread with the hungry, and to bring the homeless poor into your house; when you see the naked to cover them, and not to hide yourself from own kin? Then your light shall break forth like the dawn, and your healing shall spring up quickly; your vindicator shall go before you, the glory of the Lord shall be your rear guard. Then you shall call, and the Lord will answer; you shall cry for help, and he will say, Here I am.[59]

The Isaiah passage implies that the activity of God will be encountered not *as a consequence* of the pursuit of justice but *in* the pursuit of justice. God is not persuaded or even forced to act

---

[57] Compare, as an exaggerated example, love and hate, which operate within the same emotional framework, but in opposite directions.

[58] Cf. Amos 5.18–24, Micah 6.6–8.

[59] Isaiah 58.6–9.

by fasting or sacrifice; rather, the presence and transforming power of God is discovered in the process of ordering society with justice.[60]

JESUS THE EXPONENT OF SECOND RELIGION

I have suggested that religion appears first of all as the expression of a basic human drive to order the experience of reality through the use of ritual, symbol, and myth. First Religion wants to use that kind of knowledge to exercise control: if the sacrifice is offered properly, we will win the war; if we fast at the right time, the crops will be plentiful; if the evil eye is averted, a child will not die; if I pray hard, I will pass my examinations.

Second Religion, not less open to an infinite logic in the mystery of being, is more concerned with discovery of the divine *within*, is more committed to order for the sake of freedom than for manipulation of the divine. Second Religion is not opposed in principle to ritual, symbol, and myth, but it looks to their capacity to uncover the liberating experience of the divine. Jesus of Nazareth, who I believe was the world's clearest and strongest exponent of Second Religion, never told his followers to disregard the Sabbath (which was, after all, one of the most humane religious rituals ever invented); he did, however, tell them that the Sabbath was made for people and not people for the Sabbath, and he acted accordingly.[61]

---

[60] The imagery of God going before and after is, I suggest, drawn from the story of the Exodus. When the Hebrews first escaped from Egypt, God went before them, "in a pillar of cloud by day, to lead them along the way, and in a pillar of fire by night, to give them light" (Exodus 13.21), but when Pharaoh and the Egyptian army pursued them from behind, the pillar of cloud moved from in front of them and took its place behind them" (Exodus 14.19b).

[61] The contrast of First Religion and Second Religion is beautifully depicted in the award-winning film *Dead Man Walking*. The prison chaplain tells Sister Helen that her duty to a condemned murderer is to bring him to the sacraments so his soul may be saved and he can go to heaven. She knows that her duty is to bring him to *himself* so that he may die a whole person. The implication is clear that it is in confronting himself that he may encounter God.

It has often been fashionable in Christian circles to oppose Judaism and Christianity as though the first were a rigid form of First Religion and the second its liberating opposite. This is neither true nor fair. Second Religion, belief that the sacred (the grace and presence of God) is discovered in social and personal relationships and their integrity, and in the redeemed integrity of the individual person, is a major contribution of the Jewish tradition and not least the Hebrew prophets. However, even movements most committed to Second Religion, including Christianity, may easily slip backwards into its more primitive predecessor. The superstitious sale and purchase of indulgences to which Luther reacted is one example; so is the exaggerated reverence I was taught to pay to the physical entity of the Bible in my Protestant childhood (no other book could be placed on top of a Bible, etc.). Nothing in what follows should be understood to suggest that "good Christianity" replaced "bad Judaism." Jesus of Nazareth, as an exponent of Second Religion, criticized features of the Jewish religion of his day. He would have been equally critical of the appearances of First Religion among those who subsequently claimed to be his followers.

It is against the background of this distinction between First Religion and Second Religion that I refer to Marcus Borg's treatment of a central element of Jesus' teaching in his *Meeting Jesus Again for the First Time*.[62] Borg argues that Jesus challenged the holiness code of Leviticus 19.2, "Speak to all the congregation of the people of Israel and say to them: *You shall be holy, for I the Lord your God am holy*" (my italics). The holiness code was based on the concept of purity, not purity as merely personal cleanliness but purity as separation of God's people from the "impure" races of the world, and purity as appropriate separation within the nation itself. The Jewish nation was organized on something like a "caste" system, ranging downwards from priests and Levites, through ordinary people, converts, bastards, tax

[62] Marcus Borg, *Meeting Jesus Again for the First Time*, Harper SanFrancisco, 1994.

collectors, people with certain deformities, and outcasts (who probably included people like shepherds, whose style of life and work made it impossible for them to maintain the "pure" code of religious behaviour), among all of whom various kinds of separation were enforced.[63]

Borg argues that Jesus confronted the holiness-purity system in a number of ways: by speaking of purity as a matter of the inner state of a person ("what is inside") rather than of outer conditions or behaviour ("How blessed are the pure in heart" must be understood in these terms); by suggesting that the model of true neighbour was exemplified by the Samaritan rather than by the priest and Levite, whose obligation to the purity code made them avoid contact with what might have been a dead body; and most of all, by eating and drinking across the lines that defined the social dimensions of the code—in effect, with "dirty" people. Borg says, "In a society ordered by a purity system, the inclusiveness of Jesus' movement embodied a radically alternative social vision."[64]

Borg argues that in place of the purity code Jesus emphasized a code of compassion, paraphrasing Leviticius 19.2 as, "Be compassionate as your Father is compassionate."[65] I would suggest that although the word *compassion*, and its sister *sympathy*, are feeling-loaded words, they also carry in the agenda of Jesus the freight of appropriate action. Compassion (especially in the Greek word used by Luke) implies pity, but it does not stop with *feeling* pity. The prefix *com* means "with," and *passion* refers not only to our feelings but to the whole realm of the *passive*, to that which comes upon us, whether emotionally or at other levels of experience. *Compassion*, I suggest, means something like

---

[63] For a more cautious, thorough, and detailed treatment, see Borg, op. cit., p. 50ff.

[64] Ibid., p. 56

[65] Luke 6.36. Borg prefers "compassionate" (NEB, JB, Scholar's Version) to "merciful" (NRSV), because mercy suggests the forebearance that a higher may show to a lower. The Greek root seems closely related to the concepts of pity and compassion.

experiencing deeply with, and consequently suggests standing with others in their sufferings. It is a matter of feeling and more than feeling. This is where the sacred (holiness) is really to be found.

THE HEALING OF THE WORLD

We have already seen that Jesus expressed compassion by eating and drinking with people whom the exponents of First Religion told him were unacceptable. But he went further. He healed people, and especially across the lines of the purity code—lepers, demoniacs, epileptics, a menstruating woman, and those who were apparently dead. A personal note: ever since I came to the conclusion that the stories of the New Testament are not just magic and that they need to be reconciled in some way with the natural order as my culture has made me understand it, the healing stories have been an embarrassment to me. I have skirted around them. I have avoided them. I have welcomed suggestions that they are a later stratum of the biblical record, so I could emphasize the teaching dimension of Jesus' ministry and play down the miracles. Recent reading and reflection has made me realize that we have to work *through* the miracle stories, not *around* them.[66]

First, we have to recognize that healing is not the same as curing. Curing means the reversal of a disease, and healing may include that. But healing in the full sense of the word implies restoration of the person to full equilibrium, which includes their place in society. Again and again Jesus restores people to their proper place. When Jesus healed Peter's mother-in-law, she immediately resumed her maternal role in the household. When he healed the daughter of the synagogue leader (whom everyone thought was dead, but Jesus said was sleeping), he told the family to give her something to eat.

---

[66] I have been particularly influenced by the writings of John Dominic Crossan. I am, however, responsible for any deviations from his positions and he should not be blamed for my point of view.

Second, we must note that although Jesus is the agent in healing, he often assures those who are healed that it is *their faith*, their openness to transformation, which has made them whole.[67] In keeping with the pattern of Second Religion, such healing works from the inside out and not by an intervention from another sphere.

Third, many of the healing stories associated with Jesus have socio-political implications. Jesus' acts of healing often violated the "purity" code of his religion and culture, just like his eating with tax collectors and sinners. He challenged the accepted social fabric. Further, some of the healing stories may have had a symbolic rather than literal significance from the time of their first appearance. Is the healing of the Gerasene demoniac[68] a clinical account of an individual case or a program for regional liberation? Jesus encounters a man possessed by evil spirits, and the spirits identify themselves as "Legion," the word for a regiment in the Roman army. He casts out the evil spirits and they enter a herd of pigs and run downhill into the sea. How would we interpret a similar story if we were told that a few years ago Jesus visited South Africa, where he found a man possessed by an evil spirit who identified itself as "Apartheid," and that he released the victim from his oppression and sent the evil spirit into a pig, which then drowned itself?

We are suspicious of healing stories. They suggest snakeoil salesmen, cheap evangelists, and shrines for the credulous. We know that spontaneous remission of serious illnesses occurs, but we worry about confusing it with religious practice. We are nervous of "faith-healing," chiefly because it has a bad history, often in conflict with the patient's real and ultimate interests. As people of a scientific age (even if we are not scientists), we are more comfortable with curing than with healing. But the subject is not so easily compartmentalized. If faith is openness to transformation, and if healing is restoration to equilibrium in

---

[67] See Mark 5.34, 10.52, Luke 17.19, 18.42.
[68] Mark 5.1–20.

oneself and in one's relationships, then all psychotherapy is faith-healing. Modern medicine has become much more open to a broader view—the very concept of "family medicine" is based on the notion of maintaining a social unit in mutual equilibrium (which may include clinical intervention, but is not restricted to it) rather than on a case-by-case application of practice to a particular disease.

We cannot go back to a pre-modern notion of miraculous curing, but we can broaden our horizons to admit that a major element in the gospels is about healing as the restoration of persons and societies to mutual acceptance, interdependence, and integrity. The gospels tell us that Jesus' ministry is about the healing of the world, described by Luke (following Isaiah) in terms of good news for the poor, release for captives, recovery of sight for the blind, freedom for the oppressed, and the proclamation of the jubilee year when alienated property is redistributed.[69] The healing stories must be seen within this framework.

Mission as healing

The dismissal, the ungathering of the community, is about this mission to heal the world. At this point we must recall the gathering rite at the other end of the liturgy. I suggested that the gathering rite assembles the Christian community as an event that is the icon of God's reign. In the retelling of the Christian story, in solemn prayer of intercession, in giving thanks, and in the sharing of basic food, the kingdom of God has been been realized as paradigm, as the ultimate pattern of human life. Now the time has come to apply that pattern. The dismissal must be conceived primarily as a theological statement, and only then as a dramatic episode. The theology of the dismissal is the theology of the prophets and of the ministry of Jesus: worship is of value in so far as it shapes and enables the healing of the world.

---

[69] Luke 4.18b–19.

Perhaps the most significant Anglican theologian of the last two centuries was Frederick Denison Maurice. Maurice's major contribution was the notion that the reign or kingdom of God is not somewhere else and not beyond time, but is a present reality that it is our task to grasp in quite practical ways.[70] Maurice's theology stands behind much of modern Anglican social intervention, and more of modern Anglican theology and liturgical renewal than we may realize. In the introductory sermon of a series of addresses on the *Book of Common Prayer*, Maurice wrote,

> I hope you will never hear from me any such phrases as our "excellent or incomparable" Liturgy, or any of the compliments to our forefathers or ourselves which are wont to accompany these phrases. I do not think we are to praise the Liturgy, but to use it. If we find that it has been next to the Bible our greatest helper and teacher, we shall shrink with the modesty of piety of pupils from assuming towards it a tone of patronizing commendation. When we do not want it for our life, we may begin to talk of it as a beautiful composition: thanks be to God it does not remind us of its own merits when it is bidding us to draw nigh to Him.[71]

When we do not want it for our life, we may begin to talk of it as a beautiful composition. Maurice's warning applies to rites both old and new. If we take up residence in them, they will be our First Religion. If we use them as a manual for the healing of the world, they will be our Second Religion. The dismissal is an essential part of the liturgy because it effects the transition from

---

[70] This notion has deep biblical roots. See, for instance, Deuteronomy 30.11–14, "Surely, this commandment that I am commanding you today is not too hard for you, nor is it too far away. It is not in heaven, that you should say, 'Who will go up to heaven for us, and get it for us so that we may hear it and observe it?' Neither is it beyond the sea, that you should say, 'Who will cross to the other side of the sea for us, and get it for us so that we may hear it and observe it?' No, the word is very near to you; it is in your mouth and in your heart for you to observe."

[71] Frederick Denison Maurice, *The Prayer Book*, 3rd ed., James Clarke & Co. Ltd., London, 1996, p. 4f.

the kingdom experienced symbolically to the kingdom grasped in practice.

PRACTICAL CONSIDERATIONS

Like the opening rite, the dismissal tends to attract clutter. Extra hymns, prayers, processions, all find their way into the final moments of worship. When evensong was popular in most parishes, we used to have a remarkable form of dismissal. A blessing was said and the choir sang a solemn "Amen," often three-fold. After a period of silence, the choir processed (singing a hymn) to the back of the church, where another prayer was said and another "Amen" was sung. Then there was another silence while the candles were extinguished and the choir went off to its robing room. But often yet another prayer was said there, and from far away the congregation could hear a final, ethereal "Amen," which signalled them to quit the building.

This sentimental "oozing" out of liturgy is not helpful. The dismissal rite should leave room for the practical agenda of caring service to present itself. There is no rigorously orthodox sequence of events, but some of the following elements should be considered.

The *Book of Alternative Services* provides for silence after communion. A hymn may follow this silence, and it may be the final hymn of the assembly. (Both Matthew and Mark end their descriptions of the last supper with the words, "And when they had sung the hymn, they went out to the Mount of Olives.")

The time of dismissal is an appropriate occasion for the announcements, in which the events of the coming week may be anticipated. I suggest that the announcements should always include at least one item that relates in some way to "the healing of the world," in terms of social responsibility and concern for those who are marginalized. The liturgy then ends with prayer and a dismissal. The prayer, introduced by an invitation and brief silence, either consists of a variable prayer and an optional doxology, or a versicle and response and a text said in common.

The doxology and the prayer both have theological significance because they bridge the gap between present symbol and future practice: the doxology glorifies God, "whose power, working in us, can do infinitely more than we can ask or imagine," and the common prayer asks that the people assembled may be kept firm "in the hope you have set before us, so that we and all your children shall be free." That is what it is all about.

SECOND POSTCRIPT: LITURGY AND IRONY

I suggested in the chapter on the Prayers of the People that early Christian use of traditional terms like *priest* and *sacrifice* could have been ironic.[72] At this point I would like to go further and suggest that much of what we say in liturgy may be ironic—and with positive and creative effect.

Irony is a rhetorical or dramatic device by which we say the opposite of what we mean in order to give the meaning greater force, or describe an action whose details and results are the opposite of what we might expect in order to show the inner meaning of the events. This sounds complicated, but in fact we do it all the time.

The crudest form of irony is sarcasm. "Thank you for washing the dishes as you promised!" we may say in an unguarded moment to a neglectful teenager. Of course, the teenager has not washed the dishes and we are communicating irritation, not gratitude. Sarcasm gives our reproof a sharper edge.

Paul came close to this form of irony in his letter to the Galatian Christians, who were tempted to emulate those who wanted them to practise circumcision. "I wish," said Paul, "those who unsettle you would castrate themselves!" Did he mean that? Not literally, I suspect. He really wanted them to stop attaching undue importance to the practice of circumcision. The exaggerated irony of his remark gave it additional force—and we can feel his energy across the centuries.

There are subtler forms of irony, deeply poetic forms. In Shakespeare's *Julius Caesar*, Mark Antony in his funeral oration repeatedly refers to Brutus as, "an honourable man." It becomes apparent, however, that he is using Brutus's reputation as an honourable man against him, subtly and successfully implying that Brutus has acted dishonorably and reprehensibly. In *Antony and Cleopatra*, Cleopatra describes the asp she has procured to kill herself as, "the baby at my breast, that sucks the nurse

---

[72] See p. 51.

asleep," reversing the actual activity of the snake and interpreting death as sleep. In *Romeo and Juliet*, Juliet uses a drug to feign death, which leads Romeo to suicide because when he finds her he thinks she *is* dead. Juliet awakens and, finding Romeo's body, kills herself. Each event in the series accomplishes the opposite of what was intended, until there is nothing left but tragedy.

A subtle form of irony appears in Greek drama, which frequently consisted of traditional stories reworked by successive playwrights. Because everyone knew the story, a dramatic device was sometimes introduced that implied that the audience knew it but the actors did not, or that some actors knew it but one did not, or that the chorus knew it but the other actors did not, or some other combination of knowledge and ignorance. Once again, irony suggests that things are not what they seem and that there is unexpected meaning in the difference.

Something similar appears in the writings of the anonymous author of the second part of the Book of Isaiah. Writing in exile while his homeland and its cultic centre lie in ruins (although at a time when a political change in Babylon has introduced a ray of hope), he explores the suffering he and his people have endured. However, his most vivid description of degradation and humiliation is ultimately a veil that temporarily hides the reality of grandeur and glory. The servant who has been oppressed and afflicted and cut off from the land of the living,

> shall see his offspring, and shall prolong his days;
> through him the will of the Lord shall prosper.
> Out of his anguish he shall see light;
> he shall find satisfaction through his knowledge.[73]

Is the writer just whistling in the dark? Is he mounting a theology of false bravado? Or is he suggesting a dramatic contrast between

---

[73] Isaiah 53. 10c–11b.

present degradation and the brilliance of God's ultimate purpose? I suggest he is implying an ironic difference between present suffering and latent glory, and that the meaning of faith lies in the tension between them.

A similar form of irony may be found in John's gospel. The more Jesus reveals the wisdom of God, the more he is rejected; the more his rejection leads to humiliation, the more his hidden glory is revealed. Those who come to arrest Jesus fall to the ground when Jesus owns his identity with the words, "I am he," (words that suggest the name of God, which may not be spoken). At his trial Jesus is magisterial while Pilate fidgets and vacillates. Nailed by hands and feet to a cross and deprived of the last vestiges of human autonomy, Jesus arranges the future of his mother and his beloved disciple. Finally, he announces the completion of his task and *voluntarily* gives up his spirit (compare the synoptic gospels where Jesus' last articulate words are a quotation from Psalm 22, followed by an inarticulate cry). The glory that follows, already anticipated in the prologue as, "the glory of a Father's only son, full of grace and truth," is the opposite of the probable consequence of arrest, trial, torture, and barbaric execution. Clearly the Bible is no stranger to irony of the highest level.

Possibly the earliest Christian creed is the statement, "Jesus is Lord." This formula has attracted criticism in recent years, partly because the word *Lord* is masculine, and even more because it is drawn from language that describes a vertically hierarchical ordering of society. However, the formula takes on new meaning if it is understood ironically. In a context (like the Roman empire) of many powerful lords, both political and religious as well as human and divine, this man—who embraced vulnerability and was broken in powerlessness by the lords of "this world"—is the *true* Lord. True lordship inheres in compassion acted out for others, not in tyranny. To affirm the lordship of Christ is to stand against the power of domination and control and be on the side of the transforming power of justice and love. This fundamental expression of Christian faith, like Jesus' statement that whoever wants to be first must be last of all and servant of all,[74] is irony carried into the sublime.

Gordon Lathrop has made a careful study of early references to the eucharist as *sacrifice*, and of the appropriation of sacrificial language to Christian worship and theology. He notes that Christian liturgy (including, I suggest, Christian hymnody) is rich in sacrificial language. The words *altar, priest, temple,* and *offering* are still widely used, although Christian worship is not *sacrificial* as a Greek or a Roman, or even a worshipper at the old Jerusalem temple, would have understood that word. Lathrop analyzes a passage from the defence of Christianity that Justin presented to the Emperor Antoninus Pius around 150 C.E. Here Justin argued that God is honoured not by consuming with fire things that have been given for human sustenance but by *sacrificial liturgy* (literally "processions and hymns"—a term used to refer to important elements of non-Christian sacrificial ritual) in which they are set out with thanksgiving for the use of the worshippers and of those in need.[75] The language chosen by Justin is clearly sacrificial, but his intent is to suggest the opposite of the usual meaning of the words. The sacrifical ritual of Christians is to offer thanksgiving over food that is to be shared among the worshippers and those in need. Lathrop draws out the implications of this shift in direction.

---

[74] Mark 9.35

[75] "We have received the tradition that the only honour that is worthy of God is not to consume by fire those things which God has brought into being for human sustenance, but to set them out for ourselves and those in need, and thereby to conduct processions and hymns verbally, being thankful to God for the creation and for all the means to health, for the various qualities of the different kinds of things and for the changing of the seasons." From Lathrop, *Holy Things*, p. 144.

Justin is using metaphor, the intentional and revelatory application of the wrong words. He does this not to disguise anything, but precisely to make his point. It is as if we, living in a culture full of warfare, organized for warfare, using warfare as religion and world-view, taking warfare for granted, not even knowing a purpose for warfare anymore, would say, "These prayers we pray, these meals we eat, this food we give away, they are our 'warfare.'" We will do no other. All other warfare is utterly wrong.[76]

Lathrop has called Justin's method *metaphor*—the use of *wrong* words; I prefer to call it *irony*—movement opposite to the apparent direction.[77] I will try to illustrate this with a more or less random collection of ironic claims that Christians might have made in response to taunts and accusations from various directions.

They said to Christians, "You do not sacrifice!" And the Christians replied, "Thanksgiving for food we share among ourselves and with those in need—that's how we sacrifice." They said to Christians, "You have no sacrificial victim!" And they replied, "The crucified carpenter, who preached freedom and gave his life for his friends—*he* is the sacrificial lamb." They said to Christians, "You have no temple!" And they replied, "*We* are the *living* stones that form God's true temple." They said to Christians, "You have no priesthood!" And they replied, "We are a *kingdom* of priests." They said to Christians, "You do not honour the nation and the state!" And they replied, "We are a chosen race, a holy nation, God's own people." They said to Christians, "You are atheists who do not worship the gods." And they replied, "Everyone who loves is born of God and knows God .... If we love one another, God lives in us, and his love is perfected in us." And so on.

---

[76] Ibid., p. 146.

[77] Apart from that slight distinction in terminology, I find his argument compelling and liberating.

What we see in this process is movement from First Religion to Second Religion: the terms are the same but the thrust is reversed. It is not so much that Christianity completed the old forms of religion (in the way that a keystone completes an arch), as that Christianity (and the prophets in whose tradition Jesus stood) discerned a radically new insight in the same building blocks and in the same human field.

Unfortunately, much of the history of Christian doctrine is a chronicle of slipping back from Second Religion to First Religion, from irony to literalism, from poetry to prose (or as Lathrop might put it, from metaphor to data), followed by periods of restructuring in which reformers clawed their way back to some of the principles of Second Religion again.

How much Christian energy and unity have been lost on the question, "Is the eucharist a sacrifice?" The answer depends, of course, on the meaning of the terms. If the eucharist is understood to be a repetition of Calvary, and sacrifice is defined as a ritual action that will curry divine favour and deflect divine disapproval, the answer has to be "No." But the answer is quite different if we see the eucharist as a dramatic enactment of Jesus' mission (which involved him ultimately in rejection and death) and our commitment to follow him in his mission—that is, if we understand the whole "package" ironically as an *authentic* sacrifice, revealing the presence of God within the movement of Jesus and his followers, in distinction from the offering of animals, cereals, and even children to build a bridge to another sacred order.

We must learn to grasp the irony of the liturgy. Gathering as people without distinction of race, class, or wealth—this is our kingdom. Thanksgiving that leads to sharing among ourselves and with the hungry—this is our sacrifice. Feeding the poor in body or spirit (or making sure they are fed)—this is our priesthood.

As we approach the moment of "ungathering," the dismissal, it is important for us to be clear that our Christian sacrifice does not end when we leave the assembly. "Go in peace to love and serve the Lord" is a call to Second Religion. We have, at the table, been moulded by the paradigm once again; now it is time to apply it.

And so we go.

More than we can ask or imagine

1 More than we can ask or im - a - gine,
2 More than we will ev - er im - a - gine,
3 More than we can ask or im - a - gine,

more than we can ev - er dare to dream,
more than we will ev - er un - der - stand;
more than we could ev - er de - sire;

we are the chil - dren of heav - en's cre - a - tion,
7 we are sent to walk with com - pas - sion, to
out of the dust God's build-ing a king - dom, like

God's own be - loved, each called by name.
live out God's love by heart and by hand.
wine from the press, like bread from the fire.

And we cry, Glo - ry! *Glo - ry!* Glo - ry! *Glo - ry!*

Glo - ry to God who calls us by name!
Glo - ry to God who press-es us on! Glo - ry! *Glo - ry!* Glo - ry!
Glo - ry to God! Glo - ry we cry!

Glo - ry to God! 1 Glo - ry we sing!
Glo - ry! Glo - ry in God! 2 Glo - ry our song!
Glo - ry on earth,

3 Glo-ry on high! Glo-ry! Glo-ry! Glo-ry! Glo-ry! Glo-ry to God! Glo-ry we cry! Glo-ry! Glo-ry! Glo-ry! Glo-ry! Glo-ry on earth! Glo-ry on high! Glo-ry on earth! Glo-ry on high!

Text and music: Gordon Light. © *The Common Cup Company.*

A little child

1 A shoot shall rise from the roots of Jes - se, a branch grow up, grow strong and high. The Spir - it of God will come to rest on a lit - tle child, and de - light in the love of God shines in those eyes.

2 The ta - ble of God is set for the na - tions, for the rich and poor, for the fool - ish and wise; peo - ples and tribes will gath - er 'round to - geth - er, and de - light in the love of God will shine in their eyes. And a

3 Our name shall be be - lov - ed chil - dren, our song shall be God's free - dom cry; heart shall be the heart of the small - est child of all, and de - light in the love of God will shine in our eyes.

lit - tle child shall lead us on, the

lion and lamb   will dance as   one.   All cre-

a - tion sing   a   song   that cries out   peace,   yes,

peace!   And the   know-ledge of God   fill   the

earth,   and the   know-ledge of   God   fill   the

earth,   and the   know-ledge of   God   fill   the

earth like   wa - ters   the   seas.

Text and music: Gordon Light. © *The Common Cup Company.*